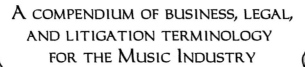

MUSIC

LAW

BUSINESS

THE
BUSINESS AFFAIRS
GLOSSARY

A COMPENDIUM OF BUSINESS, LEGAL,
AND LITIGATION TERMINOLOGY
FOR THE MUSIC INDUSTRY

SECOND EDITION

BY

ROBERT J. NATHAN

No matter what your role in the music industry, there will always be contracts to be read, deals to be negotiated, accounting reports to be examined, transactions to be reviewed, licenses to be obtained or granted, and correspondence to be dealt with. Also, in these litigious times, you are more than likely to eventually find yourself party to a lawsuit, whether you want to be or not.

Words can be a weapon or shield in knowledgeable hands. Understanding them - and particularly what they mean when used by legal professionals - can mean the difference between success and failure; between profit and loss.

Contrary to popular wisdom, what you don't know *CAN* hurt you. With that in mind, *THE BUSINESS AFFAIRS GLOSSARY* has been compiled as an elementary reference work, providing short definitions to some of the more obscure words and phrases that music accountants, lawyers, and litigators use on a more-or-less regular basis.

The Business Affairs Glossary is designed to provide definitions of certain acronyms, words and phrases commonly used in the legal and business aspects of the music industry. It is not intended as accounting, legal, business, or other professional advice, either generally or in regard to any specific instance, and it may not be taken or relied upon as such. If such advice is desired, it should be obtained from competent professionals within those respective fields. This book is intended only as an aid to comprehension of that advice.

For

Artie Mogull

(1927 – 2004)

"What are you doin'?"

ACKNOWLEDGMENTS

I want to express my appreciation to the following people for their contributions to the creation of this book:

Jillian Souza and the rest of my students in Section B of the Musicians' Institute's Music Business Program, Spring 2004, to wit; Elissa Boustani, Paul Carter, Angela Galardo, Sabrina Garner, Kara Lamb, Matt Mason, Eric Murphy, Shaun Ochsner, William Peebles, J.J. Sansone, Tobias Trapp and Jason Turitz, for urging me to begin it.

Kenny Kerner, Director of the Music Business Program, for his unflagging enthusiasm.

All of my fellow faculty members at the Musicians' Institute for the collegial atmosphere in which my efforts were nurtured.

Keight Beaven, for her assistance in proofreading the original manuscript.

And always, D. Burgundy Morgan, Esq., for her unfailing support, suggestions, criticism, late-night phone calls, and her unstoppable, cheerful attitude in the face of adversity.

- RJN

Author's Foreword

In the spring of 2004, I was teaching a course entitled *"Legal Issues and Negotiating Contracts"* at the Musicians' Institute in Hollywood. During one of my lectures, a student timidly raised her hand.

"Excuse me. But some of the 'lawyer' words you're using, I don't really understand. Is there some book I could get that would explain them?"

"Well," I replied, "Do you own a dictionary? Most of them should be in there."

"I meant, maybe, a list of the special words. Just for quick reference. Maybe you could just write a list of those for us?"

The class seemed to be in agreement that such a list was needed, and I was surprised that many of the words which confused them were not technical terms, but once-common English words with which they were unfamiliar. I had previously taught a course called *"Owning and Operating a Music Business,"* for which I'd prepared a 14-page glossary of 125 common business words and phrases, so I thought, "I'll just expand that list a little, and give them that."

So – rashly, and in a lapse of better judgment – I said, "Sure. No problem. I'll see if I can put something together for you in the next week or two."

Thus began this book.

With each new definition that I wrote, two or three additional entries came to mind. And so my "little list" grew ... and grew ... to its present length of more than 2,000 definitions. In the months which I spent writing it, I realized that it had transcended its original purpose of making my lectures intelligible to non-lawyers and had instead become a more comprehensive reference work of legal and business terms used throughout the music industry.

Because musicians' livelihoods frequently depend on documents written by lawyers working in Business Affairs departments, I felt that it might prove useful for them to have a guide to understanding certain terms which abound in those documents. (On the other hand, when I was actually in Business Affairs, the attitude was more frequently, "The less the artist understands, the better.")*

---

* The general attitude toward artists was actually *much* stronger, and not repeatable.

Of course, most artists are represented by counsel in contract negotiations, and have professional managers and accountants to consult in their business transactions, but they don't necessarily understand everything that their own advisors are saying, either.

* * *

So that's the genesis of The Business Affairs Glossary. It's intended to be a quick reference to assist musicians and songwriters in understanding the language used by music lawyers and accountants, while helping lawyers and accountants to understand artists (and each other), by providing brief definitions for legal and accounting terms unique to the music industry. I've also included a number of words and phrases that appear primarily in litigation, on the theory that it's become almost impossible to achieve success in the music industry without getting sued for something.

Bearing in mind that a dictionary is never more than an alphabetized collection of opinions, here are mine.

> — Robert J. Nathan
> Beverly Hills, California
> September 1, 2004

Introduction

"When I use a word," Humpty
Dumpty said in a rather scornful tone,
"it means just what I choose it to
mean – neither more nor less."
  "The question is," said Alice,
"whether you can make words mean
so many different things."
  "The question is," said Humpty
Dumpty, "which is to be the master –
that's all."
                              - Lewis Carroll,
                   Through the Looking Glass

Take a moment to think about the power of words.

I'm serious. Take a moment. I'll wait.

* * * * *

Now realize that your thoughts about the power of words were themselves **in words.** That little voice in your head* is speaking to you in English.

The words in which you think provide the boundaries within which you **can** think. When you learn a new word, it is merely information; but when you *master* that word – with all of its nuances and implications – you add to both the subtlety and the complexity of your own intellect. Your mental boundary is moved outward, and there is a new direction and range of thought available to you. Moreover, the process is exponential. Each newly-mastered word cross-correlates and interacts to varying degrees with all its predecessors. It is undoubtedly possible to *survive* with a limited vocabulary, but it's like wearing blinders, with vast peripheral vistas blocked off and unperceived.

"If all you have is a hammer, everything looks like a nail."

Consider your vocabulary as a toolbox. There are some tools that you use every day, while others are brought out only on rare occasions. Or there may be some that you vaguely recognize, but aren't certain exactly what they're for. The ones with which you're most familiar are used

---

*   I'm referring to the little voice that just said to you, *"What little voice? I don't have a little voice in my head. Maybe he has a little voice in **his** head, but not me."*

comfortably and with assurance. For others, you may need to refresh your memory before using them, while still others remain total mysteries and hence useless to you except as paperweights.

The problem is that you may well find yourself in a situation where those unknown tools *must* be used. But beware – they have sharp edges, pointy bits, and they can *hurt* you.

Business Affairs is a strange arena where the objective is to force the square peg of law and business into the round hole of art. This often leaves the artist uncomfortable, dazed and uncertain.

It's a much smoother process when each side understands the other's language.

Every industry has its own words of art* and the entertainment industry is no exception. Law and accountancy even more so. Artists also have their own unique vocabulary, and the curse of Babel is ubiquitous in every Business Affairs negotiation.

Many of the words and phrases in this book are purely legal terms. Please realize that lawyers *actually think in those terms!* The little voices in their heads are saying *"in pari delicto,"* while the accountants' inner voices calculate *"offsetting charges,"* and the musicians' say, *"Looks like we both screwed up."* It's the same general idea in each instance, but the internal language which each applies colors their respective thinking.

In a world where everyone thought and spoke alike, this book would be superfluous. So would music and the rest of the arts. Since we (thankfully) live in a world of diverse ideas, feel free to use this book as a cheat-sheet to translate those music industry legal, business, and accounting phrases, words and acronyms which might just bite you on the ass when you're not looking.

* * * * *

> **"Think it over! If you don't understand it, and the laws under which it will be executed, then don't sign it! — no matter how much profit may appear to be in store. Too lazy and too eager can ruin you."**
>
> **- Robert A. Heinlein**

---

* See "words of art," at Page 275, *infra.* (See p. 117 for *"infra."*)

A

@ At. Now most familiar in email addresses, the symbol was originally used (and is still used) to denote price-per-unit. *E.g.,* 12 [units] @ $14.95 [per unit]

A & R Artist and repertoire. Individuals and departments, either within a record company or operating independently, who work directly with creative artists, and who are generally responsible for signing them to a label initially, and for coordinating their relationship with the label thereafter. (See "key man clause.")

a/o "As of." Generally seen in financial reports preceding a particular date and indicating that the information contained in such report was current "as of" that date.

a fortiori An even stronger argument. With stronger reason; much more.

a priori An assumption that follows logically from a prior fact or assumption.

ab initio From the (its) beginning. An act made void *ab initio* is deemed to have never had legal effect at any time. (See also, "*nunc pro tunc.*")

abandon To relinquish with intent of never resuming right or interest.

abate To permanently stop or reduce. *E.g.,* abatement of nuisance.

abet To help someone in the commission of a crime, either before or after the fact. One who abets another is referred to as an "abettor."

abeyance Condition of being lapsed or in suspension.

above-the-line	In entertainment and production accounting, the "special" costs such as featured artist salaries, creative fees, and above-scale wages which are beyond the basic, necessary production costs. (See "below-the-line")
abrogate	To cancel or annul a provision of law, or a term or condition of agreement.
abscond	To hide, conceal, or remove oneself from a jurisdiction.
absolute	Complete, unequivocal, and without condition.
abstention doctrine	Doctrine which permits a federal court to refuse jurisdiction over a matter, relegating the litigants to another forum.
abstract	A comprehensive but abridged version of a document, delineating all of the essential elements of the original. *E.g.,* abstract of judgment.
abuse of process	Actionable misuse of legal process with an ulterior motive and for a purpose for which that process was not intended. *Cf.,* "malicious prosecution."
accede	To consent, agree or acquiesce.
acceleration clause	A contract provision which, when certain specified conditions have occurred, requires performance of obligations on an earlier date than originally agreed, or on a shortened (accelerated) schedule.
accept	To receive with approval or satisfaction. Acceptance (without condition or qualification) of an offer, plus consideration, results in a contract, under the doctrine of "offer and acceptance." Generally, acceptance is either *(a)* express (or absolute); *(b)* conditional; *(c)* implied; or *(d)* qualified.
accommodation	Arrangement made as a favor to another, without consideration in return. (See "consideration")

accord	To agree or concur. An arrangement between an injured party and the injuring party which, when performed, is a bar to all further action upon the issue between them under the doctrine of "accord and satisfaction."
accord and satisfaction	Agreement which settles all known claims between parties. Unknown claims may also be released by accord under certain circumstances, where the accord includes a specific waiver of legal protections regarding release of unknown claims. (See "release" and "known and unknown.")
accounting	*(Business)* The recording, classifying, summarizing and interpreting, in a systematic manner and in terms of money, transactions and events of a financial character. *(Law)* An equitable cause of action to judicially compel one party to account to another as to disposition of property, usually with respect to money.
accounting provision	Contract language which sets forth the manner and frequency of fiscal reports (*e.g.,* royalty statements) documenting the financial obligations between the contracting parties.
accounts payable	Trade accounts of businesses, representing obligations to pay for goods and services received. In accrual accounting, accounts payable are shown as a liability.
accounts receivable	Trade accounts of businesses, representing sums due to them for goods sold or services rendered, as reflected in notes, statements, invoices, or other written evidence of a present obligation. In accrual accounting, accounts receivable are shown as an asset, even though the money has not yet been received.
accrual	That which has accrued. In accounting, the accrual method refers to entering debits and credits on the basis of bookkeeping transactions rather than solely on an exchange of cash.
accrue	To arise, happen, come into being. To become due.

acknowledge	To admit as to a fact or, in some instances, to fail to deny a stated fact. (See "admission" and "tacit admission.")
acknowledgment	(1) An admission as to a fact or, in some instances, a failure to deny a stated fact. (See "tacit admission.")
	(2) A written statement by a Notary Public attached to certain documents, confirming the identity of the person who signed the document and that such signature was a voluntary, intentional act. (see "notary public.")
acquittal	Criminal verdict of "not guilty."
acronym	Abbreviation created by using initial (or other) letters of words included in longer phrase. Thus, "USAF" for "United States Air Force" or "ASAP" for "as soon as possible."
Act of God	Resulting exclusively from natural occurrence without the interference of any human act or agency. See also, "*force majeure*"
actionable	That which furnishes legal grounds for a lawsuit or other legal remedy.
Actors' Equity	In the United States, the union which represents actors who appear in live, dramatic stage productions, as well as the stage managers and directors of such productions. In the U.K., British Equity is the performers' union for all media (stage, TV, film and radio.)
actual notice	Notice actually received by the person being advised thereby, as distinct from "constructive notice."
actually sold	Phrase used in recording contracts to limit royalties to only those albums which have been sold to retailers and not subsequently been returned. Absent such provision, the Copyright Act requires immediate payment of publisher's royalties for all records *manufactured*, regardless of whether or not they are sold.

ad hoc	For a limited, specific purpose.
ad infinitum	Literally, "to infinity." *(Latin)* And so on, without end.
ad interim	During a period between two events. In the meanwhile. For the moment. Temporarily.
ad litem	For the purposes of legal action.
ad nauseam	To the point of nausea. Facetious reference to anything which continues to the point of making one (figuratively) ill.
ad valorem	Based on value.
addendum	An addition to a written document, added subsequently and which modifies or negates one or more of the original document's material terms. or conditions.
adduce	To determine facts from particular evidence, through reasonable inference or deduction.
adhesive contract	Also referred to as a "contract of adhesion," a contract prepared by one party which is in a vastly superior bargaining position with respect to the other party, and offered to that other party without any opportunity to negotiate or modify the contract terms. Insurance policies are classic examples of adhesive contracts.
adjourn	The final closing of a meeting or proceeding. (*Cf.*, "recess.")
adjudication	The act of giving judgment on an issue.
administering publisher	In copublishing agreements, the party who retains control over administration of the copyright and who is responsible to the other party or parties for accounting and royalty payments collected on their behalf.

administration	(1) Organization and control of a business or project.
	(2) Managing the exploitation of copyrighted works, including soliciting licensees, negotiating royalty terms, granting licenses, collecting and paying out royalties, and preparing, maintaining and delivering royalty accountings.
administrative hearing	Hearing before a governmental agency rather than before a court of law.
admiralty law	That body of law which deals with occurrences at sea. Also referred to as "maritime law" or "the law of the sea," admiralty law can become a factor in performance contracts relating to cruise ships. (See "choice of law.")
admissible evidence	Evidence which satisfies legal requirements for admissibility, and which may therefore be taken into consideration by the trier of fact in reaching a decision.
admission	Affirmation by a person that a particular statement made by another is true, or *(tacit admission)* failure to promptly deny the truth of such a statement.
admission against interest	Exception to the hearsay rule, where someone may testify as to what another person said that is contrary to that other person's interests or subsequent statements.
admit	(1) To agree that something is true.
	(2) To allow entry.
	(3) To allow particular evidence to be considered.
adopt	To take on as one's own the position or argument of another.
ADR (1)	Acronym for "alternate [or alternative] dispute resolution," referring to mediation, arbitration, or other means of peacefully resolving controversy without court trial.

ADR (2)	Acronym for "additional [or 'automated'] dialogue recording." In film and video projects, a post-production process in which performers re-record voices in synchronization with a filmed or taped image being projected for them. Generally the ADR is done by the same performer who appears in the film, but on occasion another's voice may be substituted. (See also, "dub" and "loop.")
advance	Payment made prior to the time when it is legally due. See, "advance provision."
advance man	Person who travels from location to location in advance of a tour, concert, release of an album or film, or other event, for the purpose of promoting public interest, advertising and airplay, and to make or confirm arrangements for venues and accommodations.
advance provision	Contract language which establishes the amount and due date of any advance to be paid, and which may also impose certain limitations or conditions in respect to payment, expenditure or scheduling of advances. See also, "all-in" and "split advance."
adverse	Contrary; opposite; opposed to. The opposing parties in a lawsuit (*e.g.,* Plaintiff and Defendant) are referred to as being adverse parties.
affiant	One who gives an affidavit, swearing under oath to the truth of the matters contained therein. (See also, "declarant.")
affidavit	A written document in which a person swears under oath, generally administered by a Notary Public, that the facts stated in the document are true. An affidavit is distinct from a declaration made under penalty of perjury. In some jurisdictions (*e.g.,* California) a declaration may be substituted for an affidavit for most purposes.

affirm	Confirm; agree with; approve; validate; ratify; as when an appeals court affirms the findings of a lower court. To attest that a statement is truthful.
affirmation	A solemn statement confirming that something is true. See also, "oath."
affirmative defense	That portion of an answer to a complaint which states specific legal grounds which the answering party believes will bar plaintiff's claims or will otherwise excuse the conduct alleged by the complaint on legal or factual grounds.
aftermarket	Secondary revenue sources. Purchasers of product following the period of initial marketing and primary exploitation of that product.
AFTRA	American Federation of Television and Radio Artists. U.S. performers' union representing both royalty and non-royalty singers as well as actors, announcers, comedians, narrators and sound effects artists with respect to recording sessions, radio, and live television performances.
AFM	Acronym for "American Federation of Musicians." Union of professional musicians in the United States and Canada. Also written as "A.F. of M."
age of consent	The particular age established by law on a state-by-state basis, at which a person is deemed to have acquired sufficient maturity to enter into certain agreements and to be bound by them. In most states, the age of consent is 18 years.
agency	Relationship of a person (agent) who acts for another person (principal) in certain matters.
agent	Person who is authorized to act for another in a representative capacity.

agent for service	Person who, as a matter of public record, is authorized to accept service of process on behalf of a corporation or other entity.
agreed statement	A written statement executed by adverse parties to a lawsuit, or by their counsel, agreeing that the Court may take certain matters as true for the purposes of adjudication. (See also "settled statement.")
agreement	As distinct from a "contract," an agreement is any meeting of the minds, even without legal obligation.
AGMA	American Guild of Musical Artists. Labor union that represents opera and concert singers, production personnel and dancers at principal opera, concert and dance companies throughout the United States.
AGVA	American Guild of Variety Artists. AGVA, which was the primary labor union for vaudeville performers, represents performers appearing in the United States in live variety productions that do not have a storyline or book..
airplay	Radio broadcast of commercially-released recording.
aka (a/k/a, a.k.a.)	Acronym for "also known as." An alias or pseudonym. The term is generally used after a person's true name, and before each alternative pseudonym. (See also "pka.")
akin	Related to.
album	Commercial medium (*e.g.,* a CD) containing more than two recordings. (See also "EP," and "single.")
aleatory	Uncertain; usually applied to contracts in which an obligation of one or more of the parties is conditioned upon an uncertain event, such as with insurance policies.

alias	Fictitious or assumed name which is other than the given or legal name of the person using it. Pseudonym. (See "aka" and "pka")
alibi	A defense demonstrating that a person accused of an act could not have performed that act when or where alleged.
alien	Foreign; a person who is not a citizen of the country.
alienation	Transfer of title to property, voluntarily and completely. The right of alienation – *i.e.,* the right to lawfully dispose of one's own property – is a fundamental right.
all-in	Contraction of "all-inclusive." Type of recording agreement in which the contracting party assumes responsibility for both the artist and the producer, collecting a an advance and royalties for the services of both.
allegation	A statement of purported fact asserted in a complaint.
allege	To assert a particular statement as being a true fact.
alter ego	An entity such as a corporation, organization or other structure created or operated for the benefit of another rather than (or in addition to) legitimate business purposes. Once "alter ego" has been established, the so-called "corporate veil" may be pierced, and both the entity and the individual whose alter ego it is may be held jointly and severally liable with the other for claims against either. (See also "formalities" and "pierce the corporate veil.")
alternative pleading	A legal fiction in which a common set of alleged facts may be interpreted to satisfy the requirements of more than one legal theory of recovery, and all such legal theories may be pled concurrently, in the alternative, even where a finding in favor of one theory would preclude a finding under another. *I.e.,* where a single complaint alleges both intentional tort and (in the alternative) negligence.

ambience	(1) The character or atmosphere of a particular space. (2) The general, background sound quality which is present in any particular locale. (3) The quality or character of a sound recording resulting from the space in which it was recorded.
ambiguity	That situation which exists when contract language is subject to more than one legitimate interpretation, so that its intended meaning and effect is uncertain.
ambiguous	That which is subject to two or more legitimate interpretations.
ambit	The limits or boundaries of a thing, such as a lawsuit or a jurisdiction. Thus the matters which are at-issue or otherwise relevant to an action are said to be within the ambit of that action.
amend	To alter or change by adding, substituting or removing language.
amended complaint	A complaint which replaces an earlier complaint filed by the same plaintiff against the same defendants and based upon the same general issues, although specific allegations of fact, causes of action, and legal theories of recovery may be different from the prior pleading.
American Rule	Doctrine which provides that, in the United States, each party to a lawsuit must bear the expense of its own attorney's fees unless there is a contract which specifically provides for recovery of such fees, or a statute which authorizes an award of attorney's fees for the particular cause of action pled and proven.
amicus curiae	"Friend of the court." A non-party to the action who, with court permission, files pleadings and may argue before the court upon the matter at issue. Plural, *amici curiae*.
amnesty	A broad grant of immunity by the government to one or more persons otherwise chargeable with the offense as to which amnesty is offered.

amortization	(1) A payment plan wherein periodic payments exceed accrued interest for the period, so that the loan principal is reduced by ever-increasing amounts with each payment, and the *(a)* entire loan is paid in full over a predetermined period, referred to as the amortization period (Full Amortization), or *(b)* the principal amount is reduced during that period, with the reduced amount of principal due at the time of final payment. (Partial Amortization) (2) In cost accounting, the process by which the cost of capital expenditures are spread over a number of years.
analogue (analog)	That which is functionally similar or parallel to something else, of which it is an analogue. Analogue devices are those which operate in a continuous manner, mirroring the operation of that which is being represented, recorded, or reproduced. *(E.g.,* an analogue watch mirrors the earth's rotation around its axis, in a 1-to-2 ratio; an analogue recording preserves continuous magnetic or mechanical fluctuations which parallel the sounds or images recorded.) *Cf.,* "digital."
and	This common conjunction can be of vital importance in construing legal documents, particularly as distinguished from "or."
and/or	Composite term used to indicate that elements of a list may be taken all-inclusively or only in part.
annotation (1)	Written note or comment appended to a document, either as an attached writing, or in the margins, or by interlining.
annotation (2)	A scholarly remark, note, summary, synopsis or commentary discoursing upon some portion of an opinion, statutory provision, or other writing, intended to illustrate, distinguish or explain the meaning thereof.

annotated code	Published volumes of laws which contain not only the statutes themselves, but also commentary upon each statute, including dates of its enactment or modification, legislative memoranda regarding its intention, and relevant headnotes from published opinions of courts which have applied, interpreted, distinguished, or explained that statute.
anonymous	Unidentified. Without any identification of the author. *Cf.*, "pseudonymous."
answer	A written pleading filed by a defendant in response to a complaint, in which the allegations of the complaint are either admitted or denied, and in which the defendant sets forth affirmative defenses to plaintiff's claims.
ante	A prefix, meaning "before" or "pre-" such as in "antenuptial" (before the wedding) or "antebellum" (before the war.) Used alone, *"ante"* refers the reader back to something which appears earlier in the same document.
antecedents	Ancestors. Predecessors of a person or thing. Persons, documents, property and/or other things which have preceded (in a direct, connected, or lineal manner) a person, document, property and/or thing currently under consideration.
antenuptial agreement	Written contract entered into between prospective spouses before their marriage, setting forth terms and conditions as to their respective rights and obligations regarding separate and joint property interests, income, and other business matters between them, and particularly with regard to their respective rights, obligations and entitlements in the event of a subsequent dissolution of that marriage. Also referred to as a prenuptial agreement.
anticipatory breach	Actionable conduct which occurs when one party to a contract positively states , without legal justification, an intention to not perform obligations under that contract.

apparent authority	Having the appearance of being the authorized agent of another, such that a reasonable person is justified in relying on the existence of such agency relationship. (See "ostensible agent.")
appeal	Application to a higher court to review and overrule the decision of a lower court.
appear	To submit oneself to the jurisdiction of a court, either by personally appearing before the judge, or by having an attorney make such an appearance on one's behalf, or by filing a pleading.
appearance	The act of appearing and submitting oneself to the jurisdiction of the court. Except in limited circumstances where a "special" appearance may be made, one's first appearance is deemed a "general appearance," after which the appearing party is subject to the full jurisdiction of the court throughout the pendency of the case.
appellant	One who files an appeal.
appellate	Referring to matters which are on appeal.
appellee	In some jurisdictions, one who responds to (opposes) an appeal is referred to as the "Appellee." Alternatively, such a person may be referred to as the Respondent.
appreciate	To increase in value over time.
appreciation	The amount of increase in value over time.
appurtenance	Something which is attached to real property, such as a house. Real property consists of the land itself, plus its appurtenances.
arbitrary	A decision which is not supported by substantial logic or reason.

arbitration	A semi-informal procedure for resolving disputes without going through a formal lawsuit and trial. Non-judicial arbitration is voluntary, and may be provided for within a contract from which a dispute later arises. Judicial arbitration may be court-ordered to attempt resolution before trial. Arbitration may be binding or non-binding, and in binding arbitration the arbitrator's findings and award may later be converted into a court judgment.
arbitration clause	Provision within a contract, wherein the parties agree that disputes will be submitted to arbitration (either binding or non-binding), rather than by initiating a judicial proceeding.
arbitrator	The person (or persons) who conduct and decide the outcome of an arbitration.
Arbitron	The Arbitron Company is an organization which conducts radio and television ratings research.
arguendo	Something to be assumed solely for the sake of argument, without conceding that it is true.
argument	The presentation of a particular thesis or theory, as distinct from facts and evidence.
argumentative	An objection raised in regard to a question posed to a witness, where the question is phrased in such a way as to suggest an answer favorable to the asker, or contains a statement in place of a legitimate question.
arm's length	Relationship in which the parties' respective interests are wholly distinct and separate.
arraignment	The hearing at which a criminal defendant is brought before the court to plead "guilty," "not guilty," or *"nolo contendre"* ("no contest.")
arranger	One who adapts the instrumentation and vocalization of a musical composition for performance in a manner not originally specified by its authors.

arrangement	Adaptation of a musical work which contains instrumental or vocal elements or variations not originally specified by its authors.
arrears	Money owed which was not paid when due.
art	Any expression of creative effort or activity.
articles of incorporation	Written instrument by which a corporation is initially formed.
artist	One who creates art, including music, literature, dance, painting, sculpture, photography, *etc.*
Artist	Term used in recording contracts to refer to the performer or group executing the agreement.
artist's royalties	The amount or percentage to be paid to the Artist under a recording contract, based on the number of records sold. (See, "royalty base," "SRLP" and "PPD.") Artist's royalties are separate and distinct from the mechanical royalties paid for use of a musical composition. (But see "cross-collateralization" and "single accounting unit.")
as is	In sales contracts, the statement that the subject matter is being conveyed in whatever condition it may then have, with the conveying party making no warranty as to its condition or suitability, and with the purchaser assuming all risk in regard to its usability.
ASCAP	American Society of Composers, Authors and Publishers. A performing rights organization which collects royalties on behalf of its members for the public performance and commercial broadcast use of their works. (See also "BMI," "performing rights organizations," and "SESAC.")
assault	Any willful threat or attempt to inflict injury on another, whether successful or unsuccessful

asset	Any item of property which has monetary value, including (without limitation) money itself (cash asset), accounts receivable, equipment, inventory, contracts, *etc.*
assign	To give or otherwise transfer an asset to another person.
assignability clause	Contract provision which limits the rights of a party to assign that party's rights or obligations under the contract to another person.
assignee	One to whom property is transferred by assignment.
assignment	The act of transferring an interest in property or some transferrable right to another.
assignor	One who transfers property to another by assignment.
association	A group of people or organizations joined together for a particular purpose.
assume	To take over a liability.
assumption of risk	Voluntarily and knowingly entering into a potentially harmful situation. This can include physical danger, financial risk, or other known hazards.
assumptions	(1) The act of assuming/undertaking another's debts or obligations. (2) Data assumed to be true for the purpose of progressing to a next step in reasoning
at issue	Specific matters which remain to be resolved in a dispute. Those statements which are alleged as fact by one party, but denied by another. The matters to be adjudicated in a lawsuit.
at or around	Phrase referring to a time or locale which is approximate. Also written, "at or about." (See also "on or around" and "in or around")

at source	Royalty arrangement, generally applicable to royalties earned in foreign countries, requiring direct payment of royalties to the entitled party from the foreign distributor, without passing those payments through a chain of intermediaries.
attach	To be connected to something. In planning prospective projects, those who have agreed to participate are said to be "attached" to the project, usually providing a letter indicating their commitment. (See "side letter" and "commitment letter.")
attachment (1)	Lawful (court-ordered) seizure of money or property either prior to getting a judgment, or to satisfy a judgment.
attachment (2)	Document appended to an agreement or other writing.
attorney-at-law	A licensed attorney, admitted to the bar in one or more states.
attorney-client privilege	Legal requirement which forbids an attorney from revealing any portion of communications with a client. The privilege belongs to the client alone, and may only be waived by the client, with certain narrow exceptions.
attorney-in-fact	Agent created by virtue of a "power of attorney," under which the attorney-in-fact may act with all of the authority of the principal in any matter falling within the scope of the power of attorney, including execution of legally binding documents. An attorney-in-fact may generally not appear in lieu of his or her principal in a court proceeding, but may hire an attorney-at-law to appear for the principal if the power of attorney so permits. See "power of attorney."
attorney's fees clause	Contract provision which allows for recovery of attorney's fees by the prevailing party in the event of a dispute between the parties. (See "American Rule.")
auction	A public sale of goods to the highest bidder.

audience share	Statistical percentage of current listeners/viewers tuned to a particular broadcast.
audio	Referring to a work comprised exclusively of sounds.
audiovisual	Referring to a work comprised of both sounds and visual images, such as a motion picture or music video. (See "sync license.")
audit	Examination of financial records by a trained accountant who is otherwise unrelated to the person or entity whose financial records are being examined.
auditing provision	Contract language which provides for the frequency and manner in which one party may conduct an audit of the books and records of another party to verify accurate accounting.
auditor	An accountant who conducts an audit.
authority (1)	Permission; power; A right coupled with the power to do an act, compel obedience, or otherwise exercise control
authority (2)	A legal citation of a statute or a court decision which is relevant to the case at hand and which is offered to support a particular argument as being legally sound.
authorize	To empower someone to act. To grant or delegate authority to another.
aval	A guarantee of payment.

award

Something conferred to another on the basis of merit. Monetary sum which a defeated party is required to pay to a prevailing party in litigation.

In litigation, and award is part of the judgment in the case.

In arbitration, the decision of an arbitrator, usually in the form of a written conclusion directing one party to pay a certain sum to another. Generally, in binding arbitration, the arbitrator's award may subsequently be converted to an enforceable court judgment.

B

bad faith

Intentional conduct which violates legal duty to act in good faith and deal fairly with others. (See "good faith")

bail

To release from custody in consideration of a sum of money deposited or pledged to guarantee subsequent appearance.

The sum of money deposited or pledged for such purpose.

bailee

The recipient and custodian of property received in trust from another (the bailor) as a bailment.

bailment

Property which has been placed in the custody and control of another, in trust and upon a contract (either express or implied) to perform the trust and to thereafter either return the property to the bailor, or dispose of it in a manner consistent with the trust and contract. *E.g.*, a pawn transaction or valet parking.

A bailment is created when one person (the bailee) accepts possession of another person's (the bailor's) property for a specific purpose, without any change of ownership.

bailor

One who leaves property in the custody of another (the bailee), in trust.

balance sheet

A financial statement which sets forth assets, liabilities, and net worth (equity).

bankruptcy	A condition in which a business cannot meet its debt obligations and therefore petitions a federal court under Title 11 of the United States Code for either *(a)* reorganization of its debts, or *(b)* forgiveness of debts and liquidation of its non-exempt assets. Bankruptcy may be either voluntary (initiated by the Debtor) or involuntary (initiated by creditors). See "Chapter 7," *et seq.*
bar (1)	Something which blocks or prevents something else. Thus a statute of limitations is a bar to prosecution after a specified amount of time has elapsed.
bar (2)	Literally, the railing which divides a courtroom, separating the public gallery from the court officers, parties and jurors. Attorneys are said to have been "admitted to the bar," meaning that they are court officers entitled to pass freely beyond that railing.
barratry	Instigating or aggravating disputes for the purpose of creating business for an attorney or law firm. (See also "champertry.")
barrister	In the United Kingdom, an attorney who argues cases before the court, as distinct from a solicitor who prepares the case and who practices transactional law, and who prepares cases for trial.
base price	Sum upon which artist's royalty will be calculated. In the U.S. and Canada, base price is generally arrived at by deducting an arbitrary percentage from "suggested retail list price." Elsewhere, base price is generally tied to wholesale price. See also "base price to dealers," "costs," "packaging charge," "PPD," "royalty base," "suggested retail list price," and "uplift."
base price to dealers	Term used instead of "wholesale," in some countries. Generally abbreviated by the acronym, "BPD," the term is used interchangeably with "Published Price to Dealers" and "Published Dealer Price," both of which latter terms are abbreviated as "PPD."

base royalty	Royalty percentage established in contract as being the royalty rate, but which may be subject to computational modification in specified circumstances, such as "one-half of base royalty" to be paid in respect to record-club sales. See "base price," "royalty base."
battery	Willful and actual striking of another, with intent to cause injury.
BBM	Acronym for "Bureau Benelux des Marques." See BENELUX (2).
BDS	Broadcast Data Systems. A high-tech, computerized service which constantly monitors commercial airways and, through use of recognition software, identifies the specific recordings being broadcast, reporting such usage to performing rights organizations who collect royalties on behalf of the artists.
bearer paper	Negotiable instruments (*e.g.* securities, bonds, notes) which are payable to anyone who presents them for payment.
below-the-line	In production accounting, the basic, indispensable production costs. (See "above-the-line")
bench	A general term referring to judges, as in a "bench trial" where the judge is the trier of fact, as opposed to a trial by jury. A case which is currently being tried is said to be "at bench."
beneficial interest	The right to receive some profit, distribution, or benefit, without necessarily holding (and distinct from) an ownership interest.
beneficiary	One who has a beneficial interest, as in a trust. One who is designated to receive the proceeds of an insurance policy in the event of loss.

benefit	(1) Anything which is deemed to be good for someone or something. An advantage, profit, privilege, gain, or interest.
	(2) An event conducted to raise money or other forms of support for a cause or charity.
BENELUX	(1) Acronym for the trade alliance of Belgium, The Netherlands (Holland), and Luxembourg.
	(2) The Benelux Trademarks Office, which is the official body for registration of trademarks in Belgium, The Netherlands, and Luxembourg. Interchangeably abbreviated as BTO (Benelux Trademarks Office), BBM (Bureau Benelux des Marques), or BMB (Benelux Markenbureau.)
bequeath	To give property to another under the provisions of a will.
bequest	The property given or received under the terms of a will.
Berne Convention (Berne Treaty)	International agreement (treaty) among nearly 100 countries (including the United States), governing copyright protections and remedies. Some of the treaty's requirements and protections go beyond the provisions of U.S. copyright law. See also "GATT" and "URAA."
best evidence rule	A legal doctrine which states that a secondary piece of evidence (*e.g.*, a photocopy) should not be admitted as evidence unless it can be established that better evidence (*i.e*, the original) cannot be produced.
beyond reasonable doubt	Standard of proof in criminal cases. In its traditional form, the jury is instructed that to convict they must find the defendant guilty "beyond all reasonable doubt, and to the point of moral certainty." *Cf.*, "clear and convincing," and "preponderance of evidence."
BFP	*Bona fide* purchaser [for value]. A BFP is one who acquires property in a normal and regular manner, for good consideration. (See also, "due course")

bias	Inclination; preconceived opinion. Predisposition of a judge or trier of fact toward or against a particular party. A lack of requisite impartiality and detachment.
bid	An offer to purchase or to perform for a specific, stated price.
BIEM	Acronym for *"Bureau International des Sociétés Gérant les Droits d'Enregistrement et de Reproduction Mécanique."* ("International Office of Companies Managing Fees Registration and Mechanical Reproduction") European association of agencies which sets mechanical royalty rates for Europe (excluding the U.K.) Pronounced "beem."
bifurcate	Literally, to divide into two portions. When issues in a case are tried separately from each other. *E.g.,* a seminal issue, such as a question of liability, may be tried first, with a second, subsequent trial held to determine damages if judgment in the first proceeding so requires.
bill of particulars	Written itemization of claims which a defendant in a lawsuit may demand from the plaintiff.
bill of sale	A written statement attesting to the transfer of goods from one party to another.
Bill of Rights	The first ten amendments to the United States Constitution.
binder	A written statement of the primary, material terms of an agreement. A "deal memo." Generally used as a "temporary contract," pending completion of a more formal agreement, such as an insurance policy.
black box	Fund of royalty payments received for which the proper recipients cannot be identified or located.
black letter law	A statement of law which is so well supported by legal authority as to be beyond all dispute or challenge.

Black's	Black's Law Dictionary, a standard reference work of U.S. legal terminology since 1891, currently in its 8th edition (2004).
blackmail	Unlawful demand for money or property under threat to reveal embarrassing, disgraceful or incriminating information about another, or to do bodily harm, or to damage property. *Cf.,* "extortion."
blocked funds	Monies earned in a foreign country which, under the laws of that country, may not leave its borders but must be spent there. Often, the only way to make use of these funds is through a foreign tour or purchases made in that country, or by discounting; selling an assignment of the blocked funds to someone able to purchase it with funds located outside the blocking country.
blue sky laws	Laws enacted on a state-by-state basis to protect the public from investment swindles by regulating the manner in which investment opportunities may be lawfully offered for sale.
blueback	Technically a "manuscript cover," a blueback is a piece of heavy (usually 28-lb) paper which is required to be attached to the back of pleadings filed in most federal district courts (and in some state courts). It is usually ½" wider and 1" longer than standard paper. The title of the pleading should be written on the revealed space at the bottom edge of the blueback.
BMB	Acronym for "Benelux Markenbureau." See BENELUX (#2).
BMI	Broadcast Music, Inc. A performing rights organization which collects royalties on behalf of its members for the public performance and commercial broadcast use of their works. (See also "ASCAP," "performing rights organizations," and "SESAC.")
BMG	Acronym and trade name of the Bertelsmann Music Group, a major international distributor and record label.

board of directors	Individuals, elected by stockholders, with authority to control and set policy for a corporation. Other types of organizations, such as charitable foundations, may also be governed by a board of directors.
boilerplate	In legal parlance, those documents or provisions which are used with regularity as (or in) contracts, pleadings, insurance policies or other writings, where the language changes little (if at all) from one use to the next.
bona fide	Literally "good faith." Real, authentic or reliable. Documents attesting to the authority or authenticity of someone or something are sometimes (colloquially) referred to as "*bonafides.*"
bona fide purchaser	One who acquires property in a normal and regular manner, for good consideration. More fully referred to as "bona fide purchaser for value." Generally abbreviated "BFP" (See also "BFP," and "due course")
bond	A certificate or equivalent evidence of a debt issued by a corporation or governmental body, whereby the issuer promises to pay the bondholder a specified amount of interest for a specified time, and to repay the principal sum upon a stated expiration date.
bonus	A non-refundable, non-recoupable payment which is not deducted from or credited toward earned royalties.
book value	Determination of the value of a business based upon the books and records of that business by deducting the liabilities from the assets. The book value of corporate share is determined by dividing the book value of the entire corporation by the number of issued shares.
booking	An engagement to perform at a particular time and venue.
booking agent	Person or entity (booking agency) licensed to represent artists for the purpose of securing engagements for a fee based on a percentage of the sums received for such engagement. See "talent agent."

bookkeeping	The activity of preparing and maintaining records of financial affairs.
books	The financial records of an individual, organization or project.
boycott	An organized refusal to purchase particular products or services, or to patronize particular businesses, as a means of protest and to exert economic influence in furtherance of some agenda.
BPD	Base Price to Dealers. Wholesale price. Used interchangeably with "Published Price to Dealers" and "Published Dealer Price," both of which latter terms are abbreviated as "PPD."
BPI	Acronym for "British Phonographic Institute," a trade association of record companies based or doing business in Britain.
breach of contract	Failure to perform any term of a contract which one is obligated to perform and has not been excused or prevented from performing.
breach	Literally, a tearing or a break. The failure to perform or violation of a law, right, obligation, or duty, either by commission or by omission.
breach of duty	Failure to perform that which one is legally obliged to perform -or- performance of an act which one has a legal obligation to not perform. See "negligence."
break-even point	That point in time at which the volume of sales or revenues exactly equals total expenses. (See "recoupment.")
brief	Written legal argument, generally in a format prescribed by court rule or statute.

broker	Person who arranges contracts between a buyer and seller, usually for a fee based on a percentage of the transaction. A broker may be independent, or an agent of one or more parties. (See "dual agency" and "conflict of interest.")
BTO	Acronym for "Benelux Trademarks Office." See BENELUX (2).
budget	(1) The estimated cost of a project.
	(2) A recording sold to consumers at a discounted price, frequently with a contractually-reduced royalty rate paid to the artist.
bulk sale	Sale of all or a large part of a merchant's stock as a single transaction to a single purchaser. Usually accomplished through procedures established under the Uniform Commercial Code ("UCC") to shield against undisclosed liabilities.
bullet	Iconic mark used in published charts to indicate that a recording is particularly fast-rising in sales or popularity.
bullet points	The essential and salient points of a discussion, negotiation, argument or presentation. See "deal poits."
burden of proof	The requirement that, with certain exceptions, the party asserting a claim is responsible for proving the facts supporting that claim. (Cf., *"Res ipsa loquitur"*)
business	Activity or enterprise entered into for profit.
Business Affairs	Department within a record label, production company, network, or studio which is responsible for handling contract matters. Usually staffed by attorneys and legal support personnel, the Business Affairs department may also function as a "Legal Affairs" (litigation) department in some companies.

business interruption	Type of insurance which, in the event of some circumstance which temporarily prevents a business from conducting its day-to-day affairs, pays a benefit to the business during the period of non-operation, so that the business can continue to pay its bills and payroll.
business manager	Person hired to handle another's business affairs, generally including bookkeeping, payment of bills and employee salaries, tax matters, and the retaining of professionals such as attorneys and accountants. Often, the business manager acts as attorney-in-fact under a limited power of attorney. (See "agent," "attorney-in-fact," "fiduciary," and "fidelity bond." See also, "manager" and "personal manager.")
business plan	A comprehensive planning document which clearly describes the developmental objectives of an existing or proposed business. The plan outlines the organization, resources and goals of the business, and provides an overview of the means by which the intended objectives will be achieved.
but for	Phrase used to link allegations of proximate cause and effect, asserting that "but for" some action or event, a particular result (damage) would not have occurred. A statement of causality.
but not limited to	Phrase which creates an "open-ended" list of possible, subsequent inclusions, to which anything of like or similar kind may be appended, after the fact. (E.g., "'Costs' include, but are not limited to, direct manufacturing costs." See "net") This and similar phrases (e.g., "without limitation") should be scrutinized wherever they occur, to determine if they open the door to subsequent disputes.

buy-sell agreement A contract among co-owners which provides that each must offer his or her interest to the other co-owner(s) prior to selling that interest to any third party. Also, in the event of death, permanent disability, or other specified condition affecting one co-owner, sale of that co-owner's interest to the surviving co-owners may be mandatory, pursuant to a formula or plan set forth in the buy-sell agreement. (See also, "key man insurance" and "tenancy in common.")

buyout Outright purchase of property or rights, rather than payment of royalties or licensing fees for use thereof.

bylaws Written rules governing conduct of a corporation, association, or other entity, adopted by its governing body. See also, "formalities." (*Cf.,* "operating agreement.")

C

©	International symbol for "registered copyright," usually referred to as a "circle-c." See also, "℗."
c.	Circa. *(Latin)* Around or approximately, particularly in reference to a date or point in time.
C corporation	For-profit corporation not qualified for alternative tax status under Subchapter S. (See "Subchapter S") Often referred to an abbreviated as "C-corp.")
calendar	(1) To schedule a proceeding; to set a date for an appearance. (See also, "set.") (2) The court calendar. A court's schedule of upcoming proceedings in all cases which are before that court.
cancel	Void, annul, destroy, strike, revoke and/or rescind a document or transaction.
canned	Recorded or filmed performance, as opposed to a live performance.
cap	Common term for maximum, usually established within a contract by a statement that some calculated payment, or accumulation of payments, will be for no more than a fixed sum or percentage.
capital	(1) Money invested into a venture. (2) Assets less liabilities, representing the ownership interest in a business, as well as the net worth of that business. (3) A stock of accumulated goods, especially at a specified time and in contrast to income received during a specified time period. (4) Accumulated properties capable of generating new income.

capital gains	Difference between the sale price and the original cost of property, for tax purposes.
capital expenditure	Money expended for acquisition of business equipment and/or inventory.
capital offense	Crime for which the punishment prescribed by law may include the death penalty.
capricious	Based on whim; unpredictable.
caption	That portion of a legal pleading which sets forth the name of the court, the case title, and the case number.
caption page	The first page of any pleading which sets forth the name, address and telephone number of the attorney filing the pleading, and the name of the represented party on whose behalf it is being filed, as well as the name of the court, case title, case number, and the title of the pleading.
care	To be attentive, prudent and vigilant. Fulfilling those basic duties that are normally associated with one's position. A fundamental duty of all people.
CARP	Copyright Arbitration Royalty Panel, a body operating under the authority of the Library of Congress ("LOC") to set and adjust royalty rates, to distribute royalties deposited with the LOC to copyright owners, and to conduct hearings to resolve copyright disputes. The CARP has supplanted the former Copyright Royalty Tribunal.
case of first impression	Case which presents a question of law which has not been previously interpreted in a published case.
case law	Reported decisions of courts, which are used for authority to guide and justify actions of later courts in ruling upon similar issues.

cash flow	(1) The overall comparison between monies received and monies expended. When income exceeds expenditures it is referred to as a "positive cash flow." Expenditure greater than income results in "negative cash flow."
	(2) An accounting report, summarizing and comparing expenditures and income over a specified period of time.
cashier's check	Check issued by a bank payable from its own accounts.
casual	That which happens by chance, rather than by design.
catalog (catalogue)	(1) Collection of master recordings owned or controlled by a record company or other entity.
	(2) Collection of copyrights owned or controlled by a songwriter, publisher, or other entity.
cause of action	That portion of a lawsuit which sets for a specific legal theory *(e.g.* breach of contract; fraud; common counts), and enumerates the essential elements which, if proven, comprise all necessary elements to support recovery under that theory.
caveat	A warning. Literally, "beware!" *(Latin)*
caveat emptor	"Let the buyer beware." Doctrine which imposes a duty on the purchaser to be diligent in determining the worth and potential defects of that which is purchased. The doctrine has been significantly diluted by consumer protection and product liability laws.
CD	(1) Acronym for Compact Disc.
	(2) Acronym for Certificate of Deposit.
CEO	Acronym for "Chief Executive Officer," of a corporation or other organization. (See, "president.")

certificate	A written document originating from some governmental, educational, organizational or other authority, attesting that some act has or has not been completed, or that some legal or other formality has been concluded, or some honor conferred.
certificate of deposit	A type of savings account which yields higher interest than that of passbook accounts, but with a requirement that the funds remain untouched for a fixed period of time, and with penalties (which effectively negate earned interest) in the event of an early withdrawal of funds.
certified copy	Copy which has been made by a government official from the filed original of a document, and which bears a signed certificate and appropriate stamps and seals, attesting that such copy is absolutely identical to the original on file.
certified public accountant	A licensed, professional accountant (in the United States). Generally abbreviated "CPA."
certify	To attest, although not necessarily under oath or penalty of perjury, that some representation is true, or that some formality has been completed, or that some other act has or has not been done.
certiorari	Writ issued by a higher court to a lower court, requiring the lower court to produce all records of a proceeding for review by the higher court. Certiorari is obtained through a petition filed in the higher court by an interested party.
cf.	Abbreviation for Latin "confer." Often read as "but see," or "compare with" indicating that there is additional, relevant, differing matter which should be considered.
CFO	Acronym for "Chief Financial Officer," of a corporation or other organization. (See, "treasurer.")

chain of custody	Succession of persons having actual possession of evidence, in unbroken sequence from time of its origination or collection until its presentation in court. Where an unbroken chain of custody cannot be established, evidence may be subject to exclusion. (See "foundation." *Cf.*, "exceptions to hearsay rule.")
chain of title	Succession of title ownership to property from one owner to the next, in unbroken line.
chair	(1) Abbreviated form of chairman, chairwoman or chairperson. The person who presides at a meeting or proceeding, and who is generally the most senior of the people participating. (2) To preside at or conduct a meeting or proceeding. (3) In litigation, a reference to the attorneys who participate in trial, usually to distinguish the lead attorney (first chair) from attorneys who assist him or her (second chair, third chair, etc.)
chambers	Judge's private office, usually adjacent to the courtroom. Some proceedings are held "in chambers," either on or off the record.
champertry	Maintaining, supporting, financing, or promoting the lawsuit of another. (See "Barratry")
change of venue	The moving of a court proceeding from one location to another court or county, usually for the purpose of avoiding prejudice to a criminal defendant, or for the convenience of witnesses.
Chapter 7	Bankruptcy. Governed by Title 11 of the United States Code ("USC"), Chapter 7 of that Code [*i.e.*, 11 USC §§ 701-766] regulates the liquidation of a bankrupt estate, where any non-exempt assets are sold for the benefit of creditors, and the debtor becomes debt-free (subject to certain non-dischargeable exceptions such as taxes, student loans, spousal support, and specifically listed tort liabilities, *etc.*, for which the debtor remains liable.)

Chapter 11	Business reorganization in bankruptcy. Procedure provided by Chapter 11 of Title 11 of the United States Code [11 USC §§ 1101-1146], whereby all prior debt is held in abeyance so that the debtor can continue to operate its business while paying all newly-created obligations and developing a business plan to satisfy its old debt. If such a plan cannot be developed, or fails, the Chapter 11 may be dismissed or converted to a Chapter 7 liquidation. (See "Chapter 7.")
Chapter 13	Personal reorganization in bankruptcy. For qualified individuals with regular income, Chapter 13 of the United States Code [11 USC §§ 1301-1330] provides relief similar to that of Chapter 11, but on a more streamlined and expedited basis, allowing the debtor to adopt a plan for full or partial payment of old debts, while continuing to pay all current and new obligations. If the debtor fails to file or complete the plan, the Chapter 13 may be dismissed or converted to a Chapter 7 liquidation (See "Chapter 7," and "Chapter 11.")
character witness	Person who testifies at trial as to the character or habits of another person, rather than as to the facts of the case.
charge	A specific statement of a particular crime alleged against a criminal defendant. The criminal-case equivalent of a "cause of action" in civil pleading.
chargeback	Record company expense item (*e.g.,* advances, studio fees, producer fees, *etc.*) deducted from royalties payable to artist. See, "recoupment."
chart	(1) List of commercial recordings published in trade papers, organized in descending order of current popularity. Each genre of music is generally listed separately, and "popularity" is based upon radio airplay and/or record store sales. (See "bullet.") (2) To have one's recording appear upon such charts.

charter	Document by which a sovereign government (*i.e.,* a state or nation) grants rights to a person or group. In current (U.S.) usage, charters primarily appear as an official document confirming the formation and existence, and enumerating the rights and powers, of a corporation, particularly including public corporations such as municipalities. (See "public corporation.")
chartered accountant	In the U.K., a licensed (*i.e.,* chartered) professional accountant.
chattel	An item of personal property which is movable, as distinct from real property, appurtenant property, and intangibles.
chattel paper	Document providing for a security interest in tangible, moveable property. See "UCC-1."
chill	To cause a reduction or withdrawal of enthusiasm or support.
choice of forum	Contract provision by which the parties stipulate as to the jurisdiction in which any dispute between them will be resolved or adjudicated.
choice of law	Contract provision by which the parties stipulate as to which jurisdiction's laws will govern interpretation and enforcement of that contract or of other, specified issues.
choice of law and forum	Generally, choice of law and choice of forum provisions are integrated into a single contract provision, which may also address conflict of laws and attorney's fees issues. (See "attorney's fees clause" and "conflict of laws.")
circa	Around or approximately, particularly in reference to a date or point in time. *(Latin)*
circumstantial evidence	All evidence other than eyewitness testimony.

citation	Reference to the published decision in another case, or to a statute or other legal authority.
cite	To refer to the published decision in another case, or to a statute or other legal authority.
civil	That aspect of the law which governs private rights and remedies, as contrasted to criminal matters. Civil law addresses business, contracts, personal injury, and virtually all non-criminal matters involving persons. (*Cf.* Admiralty law, Military law, *etc.*)
civil procedure	Body of laws, rules and regulations governing the means and manner in which civil claims may be presented, prosecuted, defended, tried and adjudicated. Rules are similar-but-different in each jurisdiction. There are Federal rules of procedure (F.R.Civ.P.), state statutes and rules for each state, local rules for each state and federal judicial district or division, and each court may also have its own rules.
claim	A demand for money, for property, or for enforcement of a right.
class action	Lawsuit filed by one or more people on behalf of themselves and on behalf of others not specifically named but who are similarly situated to the named plaintiff(s) and who are alleged to have been similarly damaged by the same conduct complained of. Once filed, the court must determine if a true class exists.
clause	Separate and specific language appearing in a contract or other writing. Generally, the words "provision" and "clause" may be used interchangeably in referring to contract language, although technically a "clause" is a general term of a contract, whereas a "provision," relates to a potential occurrence. (See also, "provision.")

clean hands doctrine	A legal doctrine which states that a person coming to court with a suit must be acting in good faith and that the complaining party's prior conduct with respect to the matter at issue has not violated equitable principles or conscience. See "unclean hands."
clear title	Holding a legal ownership interest which is unclouded by any conflicting claims.
clear and convincing	The higher of two standards of proof in civil cases. Under this standard, the evidence must be sufficient to satisfy the trier of fact that there is good and sufficient evidence to support a particular conclusion. (See "burden of proof" and "preponderance of evidence.")
clearance	Permission to use a copyrighted work, with or without payment.
clemency	Mercy. An official modification of a court-imposed sentence, clemency may be granted to the convicted offender by the executive authority of a state governor (for state crimes) or the President (for federal crimes), reducing it to a lesser term or form of punishment. See also, "pardon."
close corporation	A corporation which is owned by a limited number of shareholders, generally no more than 35 and as few as 1. See "Subchapter S corporation."
closing argument	Summation of evidence presented, and argument as to conclusions which may be drawn from that evidence, offered by counsel at the conclusion of trial, before deliberation and verdict.
cloud on title	A claim, usually recorded on the title record, which challenges the clear title of the owner-of-record. *E.g.* a mechanic's lien.
CMRRA	Canadian Musical Reproduction Rights Agency, Ltd.. A non-profit music licensing agency which represents music publishers doing business in Canada.

coalition	A temporary alliance, usually for a particular purpose.
coauthor	One who creates an artistic work together with one or more others. Absent an agreement to the contrary, coauthors each share an equal, undivided interest in the whole work, and any coauthor may grant a non-exclusive license to record, manufacture, perform or otherwise exploit the work without the consent of the other coauthors, providing that sums received for such license are distributed equally among all the coauthors.
co-insured	One who, under an insurance policy, is designated to receive joint payment with another in the event of a covered loss.
code	Body of written laws created by legislative authority, setting forth specific requirements of conduct. Codes are generally divided into those areas of law which they particularly address, such as criminal matters (Penal Code), civil matters (Civil Code), procedural matters (Code of Civil Procedure), *etc.*
Code of Napoleon	See "Napoleonic Code."
codicil	Written, executed and attested amendment to a will.
codify	To establish and organize a system of written laws, or to embody a legal principal as a written law.
cogent	Convincing; well reasoned; logically related and material to the matter at hand.
cohabitation	Two or more persons living together, generally as husband and wife or in a similar type of relationship.
collateral	Something of value pledged to support the repayment of an obligation. (See also, "bailment.")
collateral document	A legal document covering the item(s) pledged as collateral on a loan, i.e., note, mortgages, assignment, etc.

collateral estoppel	A situation in which the ruling of a court in one case prevents (*i.e.,* estops) the court in another case from making a contrary ruling upon an identical issue respecting the same parties. See also, *"res judicata."*
collective work	For copyright purposes, a work in which a number of separate and independent works are joined into a collective whole, and registered as such.
collective bargaining	Employment contract negotiations between employer (or group of employers) and union representatives and group of employees, to reach agreement on future terms of employment .
colloquy	A conversation, generally formal in setting and tone. A written dialogue. An informal or theoretical discussion between attorneys and judge, either on- or off-record.
colloquial	Relating to conversation; conversational. As used in common speech.
collude	To conspire or to act in concert with another in a manner or for a purpose inconsistent with law.
collusion	Two or more persons agreeing between themselves to act jointly in a manner inconsistent with law.
collusive action	A lawsuit brought by parties against one another, purporting to be adversaries but, in fact, acting in concert with each other for the purpose of obtaining a disposition ultimately favorable to them both, often unfavorable to persons not party to the suit.
color of authority	Those acts performed or authorized by a public official in apparent fulfillment or furtherance of his or her official duties.
color of law	Acts performed or authorized by a public official or police officer in apparent enforcement of a law or statute. That which has the appearance of being performed in accordance with legal authority.

color of title   The appearance of having legal title to property.

colorable   That for which a viable argument exists.

comity   Respect; deference; courtesy. When one court defers to another not as a clear matter of right but out of courtesy and good will. The doctrine also applies to other branches of government, to states, and to sovereign nations.

commercial law   That body of law which relates to the conduct of business and commerce. (*Q.v..*, "Uniform Commercial Code")

commingling   A mixing together of funds belonging to one distinct entity with those belonging to another. The use of business funds for personal expense, and *vice versa*, such that the separateness of the two become indeterminate. (See "pierce the corporate veil.")

commission   (1) A fee based on a percentage paid to a person for a service rendered in connection with a transaction.
(2) Delegation of authority to act for express purpose.
(3) Group of persons acting pursuant to delegated authority.

commitment   (1) Condition of having agreed to participate in or support a particular undertaking. A pledge of support.
(2) An obligation which restricts freedom of action.
(3) Court order transferring someone to jail or prison upon conviction, or which sends a person into some other form of institutional custody.

commitment letter   A written promise to participate in or support a particular undertaking or project. See also, "inducement letter" and "side letter."

common counts   A cause of action for collection of money owed.

common law	Body of law, both written and unwritten, which originated in England and which forms the general basis for most American jurisprudence. Common law is derived from ancient usage and custom, and from the decisions of courts interpreting such law over centuries, and is distinguished from statutory laws which have originated through legislative acts.
common property	(1) Property owned by more than one person (See, "tenants in common.") (2) Property in condominium projects and certain developments which is deemed a "common area" and is undividedly owned in common by all the property owners.
common stock	Basic shares in a corporation, generally as distinguished from "preferred stock."
community property	Property and profits received by a husband and wife while married, subject to certain exceptions which are deemed "sole and separate property" of one or the other.
commutation	Reduction of a criminal sentence, after the fact, by executive order.
comp (1)	Colloquial abbreviation of "complementary." Admission and/or other amenities provided at no charge to an invitee, generally for promotional purposes.
comp (2)	Colloquial abbreviation of "comparative price."
compact	(1) A mutual agreement between persons, states or nations, generally setting forth common goals with respect to some issue or venture and the manner in which they will cooperate jointly in that regard. (2) Small; of reduced sized. (3) To compress into a smaller size.

compact disc (CD)	Circular (120-mm.) recording medium capable of storing digital data, and from which sounds and other information can be retrieved and reproduced through use of a laser.
company	Any business entity operated with the intent to obtain profit thereby.
comparative negligence	A doctrine used primarily in accident cases to determine the percentage of responsibility of each person involved, for the purpose of reducing overall damages, *pro rata.*
compensation	Payment received for work performed, by salary, wages, commission, or other consideration.
compensatory damages	Award of monetary damages deemed equal to the actual injury suffered.
competent	Capable of acting effectively in the circumstances. Having the capability to understand and participate.
compilation	A work formed by compiling preexisting recordings into an order or arrangement which constitutes an original work of authorship. Compilations include collective works. (See also, "derivative works.")
complainant	One who files a complaint. (See also "Plaintiff")
complaining witness	Alleged victim of crime who testifies against accused.
complaint	Written document setting forth claims alleged by one or more persons (Plaintiffs) against one or more other persons (Defendants), filed with the clerk of the court, thereby initiating a lawsuit.

compliance clause	Contract provision requiring signatories to comply with particular requirements of law or provisions of a separate agreement, generally a collective bargaining agreement. In recording contracts, the artists are generally required to be active members of the appropriate performers' union (*e.g.*, AFM, AFTRA.)
compos mentis	"Of sound mind." Hence, "*non compos mentis,*" as referring to one who is not of sound mind.
composer	Author of a musical work, or of the musical portion of a song. When a song is written contemporaneously by a composer and lyricist, they each share equally in the indivisible whole, with each considered a coauthor of the other's contribution, unless there is a specific agreement between them to the contrary. (*Cf.,* "lyricist." See also, "songwriter.")
compound question	Objectionable form of question in which two or more distinct questions are stated within what would appear to be a single question.
compound interest	Interest periodically calculated as a percentage of both principal and all previously accrued interest. *Cf.* "simple interest."
compounding a felony	Offense of accepting payment or other recompense in consideration of not reporting or prosecuting a crime.
compromise	Agreement between opposing parties to settle a dispute upon particular terms.
compromise verdict	An impermissible decision by a jury in which the jurors "split the difference" between them to conclude deliberations, rather than voting their respective consciences.

compulsory license	Provision of copyright law which permits artists to record another's composition and pay a monthly, statutorily-set royalty for such use at any time <u>after</u> the composition has been previously recorded and distributed as a phonorecord. See, "first use," "mechanical license," "phonorecord" and "statutory rate." *Cf.,* "incept license."
concealment	Failure to disclose information about a matter. When the matter is material (*i.e.,* important) and the person concealing it had a duty of disclosure to a damaged party, concealment may be actionable as a fraud.
conclusion of law	Statement of judge's opinion and determination on a question of law which has been presented in the course of proceedings.
conclusion of fact	Statement of judge's opinion and determination on a question of fact which has been presented in the course of proceedings.
concurrent	At the same time.
condemnation	Legal process whereby a government body deems a structure unfit for continued use. See "imminent domain."
condemnation action	Lawsuit brought by a public agency to enforce condemnation of private property.
condition	(1) Requirement stated in a contract which must be fulfilled as a material term of the agreement. (2) A proposed, required term or provision. (3) A circumstance which exists. (4) The fitness, health, or general functionality of a person or thing.
condition precedent	That which is required to occur before a subsequent thing may occur.

condition subsequent	That which is required to occur after a previous thing has occurred.
conditional delivery	Delivery which is made only upon the recipient's agreement to accept certain terms. (See "offer and acceptance.")
conditional sale	Agreement in which sale of property or goods will conclude upon completion of one or more specified conditions.
condominium	A form of real property ownership in which one exclusively owns a specified portion of a larger property, plus an undivided fractional interest in common areas of that larger property.
condone	To overlook, forgive, support, and/or allow actions of another which are inconsistent with law or moral principles.
confess	To voluntarily state that one is guilty of having committed a specified wrongful act.
confession to judgment	A written declaration by which an indebted person acknowledges the debt and expressly authorizes the creditor to obtain a court judgment against the debtor without having to file a lawsuit to prove the debt.
confession	Statement in which one confesses, generally to a crime. Also, one of the exceptions to the hearsay rule, under which testimony otherwise improper will be admitted to allow a third party to testify that an accused has confessed in the hearing of that witness.
conflict	A situation in which the intentions, ideas or interests of two or more persons or groups are inconsistent with each other or are mutually exclusive.

conflict check   Preliminary research conducted by an attorney or firm to determine if representation of a new, prospective client, creates a conflict of interest with respect to any prior client and therefore precludes accepting employment from the new client with respect to a particular matter.

conflict of interest   Situation in which a person has a duty to two or more others whose interests conflict with each other's, such that the person owing the duty cannot act for one without breaching duty to another. Some conflicts can be waived, by disclosing the conflict to all affected parties and obtaining their express consent to proceed notwithstanding the conflict. Certain types of conflict cannot be waived, as a matter of law. Such conflicts are referred to as being "irreducible."

conflict of law   Situation in which the laws of two or more states or federal law are inconsistent upon the same subject. Contracting parties may stipulate as to which body of law will govern interpretation and disputes provided that there is no overriding public policy or legal doctrine to the contrary. (See "choice of law.")

conformed copy   Copy of a filed document, bearing a stamp affixed by the court or agency where the original was filed, at the time of filing. (Note: a conformed copy is not the same as a "certified copy.")

confusingly similar   A determination that a trademark, service mark, trade name, logo or other marketing materials of one entity is so like that of another that a reasonable person might readily confuse them and patronize one while believing it to be the other. See "Lanham Act" and "unfair trade practices."

consecutive   Following continuously and in sequence.

consent decree   A court order based upon an agreement between parties to resolve an issue.

consent   Acceptance. Voluntary agreement to another's proposition.

consequential damages	Special damages which are sometimes awarded in a lawsuit for expenses incurred as a readily traceable consequence of defendant's actions, although not proximately caused by such actions.
consideration	An element of contracts, consideration is that which one party gives to another (*e.g.,* money) in exchange for the consideration received from that other party (*e.g.,* goods or services.)
consignee	The person or business holding another's goods for sale on consignment.
consignment	A type of merchandising arrangement whereby goods are delivered to a merchant without payment, and those goods are then offered for sale, after which sale the consigning party is paid the sale price, less a commission to the merchant. (See also "bailment")
consolidation	Joining together of two or more related actions so that they may be adjudicated by the same judge, usually at a single trial. Consolidation avoids inconsistent rulings upon identical facts.
consortium	A coalition of organizations, such as banks and corporations, set up to fund ventures requiring large capital resources.
conspiracy	Two or more people working in concert, by common agreement, for an illegal purpose.
conspirator	One who participates in a conspiracy.
constitution	The fundamental, underlying agreement which forms the foundation for all laws and governmental operations.
constitutional rights	Rights enumerated in, or which may be judicially inferred from, the Constitution and its amendments.

constructed price	Arbitrarily established but fictitious price used to calculate royalties for territories which do not allow SRLP or fixed PPD.
construction	The act of interpreting, analyzing, and determining the intended meaning of a legal writing such as a contract or statute.
constructive	A legal fiction, wherein something is deemed to have occurred by operation of law, although it may not, in fact, have actually happened.
constructive notice	A circumstance where, by reason of publication, recordation, posting, notification to an agent, or other means specified by law, affected persons are deemed to have received adequate notice, even though they may, in fact, never have received actual notice and been wholly unaware of the matter noticed.
constructive trust	A legal theory wherein a person who has obtained property through wrongful acts is deemed to hold it only as the involuntary trustee of the rightful owner, for that true owner's benefit.
construe	To determine the meaning of the words of a written document, such as a contract or statute. (See "construction.")
container charge	A percentage or fixed sum deducted from the retail price (SRLP) of a recording before calculating artist's royalties, on the theory that certain tangible portions of the final commercial product do not result from the artist's creative contribution. Also referred to as a "packaging" charge or fee. The container charge is customarily 25% of SRLP. See also, "packaging charge."
contempt of court	Conduct which is disparaging of the authority or decorum of a court, contempt may be either direct contempt (*i.e.* contemptuous conduct within the court or chambers) or indirect contempt (*e.g.*, willful violation of a court order.)

contiguous	Referring to two or more parcels of real property which share common line of boundary between them. Adjacent.
contingency	Some eventuality which might not occur, but for which some pre-planning is nonetheless prudent.
contingent	That which is possible, but not certain.
contingent liability	A potential obligation that may be incurred dependent upon the occurrence of some future event.
contingent fee	An attorney/client fee arrangement, where the attorney receives payment if, and only if, he achieves a successful outcome for the client. Generally, such fees are based on a percentage of recovery rather than upon the time expended.
continuance	Court-ordered postponement of the date of a court proceeding.
contra	Literally "against" or "opposite to." Generally used to identify a proposition or authority which differs from that which precedes it. Used similarly to the phrase, "On the other hand..."
contract	An agreement between two or more competent persons with a discernable objective, specified terms, common understanding, mutual consideration and mutual obligations. A contract is formed once there has been an offer, unconditional acceptance of that offer, and any manifestation of consideration.
contract of adhesion	See "adhesive contract"
contractor	One who performs services for another, not as an employee but as an independent business venture.

contribution	(1) Something given to help achieve some particular purpose. (2) Legal action to require co-obligors to perform their respective share of an obligation.
contributory negligence	A legal doctrine and affirmative defense which states that where plaintiff's injury proximately results in part from plaintiff's own lack of due care, defendant's liability may be reduced accordingly.
control	The authority to direct, manage and restrict an entity, property, or instrument.
controlled compositions clause	Provision in recording contracts whereby the record label avoids or reduces its obligation to pay mechanical royalties on compositions controlled by the recording artist.
controlling law	That body of law, whether state, federal, or that of a foreign nation, which is deemed to be the law under which a matter will be tried or under which an instrument will be interpreted. (See "choice of law" and "conflict of laws.")
conversion	A tort (civil wrong) in which one takes (converts) another's property and uses it for the taking party's own benefit. Conversion is the civil equivalent of the criminal charge of larceny or theft.
convey	To transfer ownership of property to another.
conveyance	A written instrument (*e.g.,* a deed) which transfers ownership from one person to another.
convict	(1) To find someone guilty of a crime. (2) One who has been convicted of a crime.
COO	Acronym for "Chief Operating Officer," of a corporation or other organization.

co-publishing (copublishing)	Copyright situation in which two or more entities share publishing income (royalties and licensing fees) although not necessarily the publishing responsibilities.
copyright	Limited monopoly establishing the exclusive right of the creator of a work of literary or artistic nature to control the publication and copying of that work. Copyright exists from the moment that a work is first embodied in tangible form, although registration is necessary to allow for claims under copyright law (Title 17 of the United States Code). The specific rights protected by copyright are: (1) The right to reproduce copies of the work; (2) The right to distribute the work; (3) The right to control derivative works; (4) Public performance rights; and (5) Public Display rights. Additionally, the right of "first use" with respect to the enumerated rights is inherent. (*Cf.* "compulsory license.")
copyright, duration of	Copyright in a work created on or after January 1, 1978, endures from the date of its creation for a term ending 70 years after the death of the last surviving author, unless the work is anonymous, pseudonymous, or a work for hire, in which event the copyright endures for a term of 95 years from the year of its first publication, or a term of 120 years from the year of its creation, whichever expires first. (17 U.S.C. § 302)
Copyright Arbitration Royalty Panel	U.S. governmental body (replacing the former Copyright Royalty Tribunal) operating under the authority of the Library of Congress ("LOC") to set and adjust royalty rates, to distribute to copyright owners' royalties deposited with the LOC, and to conduct hearings. Generally abbreviated "CARP."
Copyright Board of Canada	Agency of the Canadian government which establishes royalty rates for copyrighted works.
copyright registration	The act of recording one's claim of copyright ownership with a government agency. In the United States, such registrations are accepted by the Copyright Office of the Library of Congress.

coroner	County official charged with responsibility for determining and officially declaring cause of death of persons who die within the coroner's jurisdiction, as well as other legal and *quasi*-police duties.
corporation	A legal entity created by issuance of a governmental charter recognizing its separate existence, rights, privileges, and liabilities distinct from those of the person(s) owning or controlling it. A corporation is a separate "person" under the law. (See, "legal fiction.")
corpus	Literally, "body." *Corpus* is generally used to denote the substance of a thing, such as assets comprising the *corpus* of a trust.
corpus delicti	The substance or foundation of a crime, or the substantial fact that a crime has actually been committed.
corpus juris	The body of law, used to refer to a compendium of all applicable statutes and court decisions.
corroborate	To confirm or substantiate the statement of another.
corroborating evidence	That which confirms, strengthens, adds to, or validates other, previously-introduced evidence.
costs	Money obligation for goods and services received. In the recording industry, expenditures designated as "costs" are generally subject to recoupment by deduction from Artist's royalties.
cotenancy	A circumstance where more than one person has an ownership or separate contractual interest in a single property. Tenants in common.
coterminous	(1) Having a common point of termination. Coterminous contracts are agreements which both end when either one is terminated, for any reason. (2) Having a common boundary, such as adjacent properties.

count	Each separate statement in a complaint which states a distinct cause of action or claim for relief.
counterclaim	Claims for affirmative relief made by a defendant against a plaintiff, in response to plaintiff's complaint. (See "cross-complaint")
counterfeit	Forged; false; an imitation. To make or copy without license or right.
counteroffer	An offer made in response to a different offer with respect to the same subject matter. Part of the process of negotiation leading up to a contract.
counterparts	In contract law, two or more identical documents, each bearing the signature of fewer than all necessary signatories, but when taken together containing all of the necessary signatures.
coupling	Joining two or more recordings that were not originally recorded or released together, generally using recordings by different artists. (See also, "compilation")
course of employment	Those activities which are normally, customarily or necessarily within the scope of one's job.
course of business	Those activities which are normally, customarily or necessarily within the scope of a business' operations.
court below	In appellate pleadings and opinions, phrase used to refer to the lower court whose decision is being appealed.
court costs	Certain expenses of litigation, such as filing fees, witness fees, court reporter's fees and other, similar items, which are generally recoverable by the prevailing party upon judgment.
court	Forum, presided over by a judge, magistrate, or commissioner, in which disputes are heard and resolved by operation of law.

court of appeals	A court which reviews judgments or rulings of a lower court, with the power to correct errors of law.
court calendar	List of matters which are scheduled to be heard or tried before a particular court, and the dates upon which hearings or trials are set.
court trial	Trial with a judge but no jury, also referred to as a "bench" trial.
court-martial	A military court which tries offenses under military law.
covenant	An enforceable promise, generally memorialized within a contract or recorded instrument.
cover	(1) A recording made of a composition previously recorded and released by another artist.
	(2) The packaging in which a recording is released for sale, generally with artwork and text printed on it.
CPA	Acronym and common abbreviation for Certified Public Accountant.
creation	The act of bringing something into existence for the first time. In copyright law, the copyright exists from the moment of creation, although registration of that copyright is a prerequisite to prosecuting a court action for infringement.
creative	That which is capable of acts of creation. Inventive; innovative; artistic.
creative accounting	Facetious reference to bookkeeping practices which seek to maximize profit, overstate assets, and/or understate liabilities. In the entertainment industry, "creative" accounting practices have frequently been used to reduce an artist's "net" by narrowly defining "income" (or "revenue") while broadly interpreting "costs" and "expenses." (*Cf.,* "GAAP")

Creative Commons Nonprofit corporation that enables artists and authors to register and licence their creative works online.

creative control Right to make final determinations as to the artistic content and elements of a project. This right naturally vests in the artist, but is assignable to another, by contract.

Creative Director The person in charge of creative services for a record label or production company.

credibility A determination as to whether testimony is worthy of being believed.

credible witness A witness whose testimony is perceived to be true.

credit (1) Attribution of creative contribution, generally appearing on the face of a recording and/or in printed material which is sold with that recording.
(2) An accounting entry, indicating that an amount is owed.
(3) An amount owed which is generally only collectible in the form of future goods or services.
(4) Privilege of obtaining goods or services before payment, based on trust that payment will be made.

credit rating A score assigned to a business concern to denote the net worth and credit standing to which the concern is entitled in the opinion of the rating agency as a result of its investigation.

creditor A person or entity to whom a debt is owed.

crime Actual or constructive injury to the public, in violation of law and for which the law specifies criminal penalties. Crimes are generally divided into felonies and misdemeanors.

criminal General term for anyone who has committed a crime, whether felony or misdemeanor.

criminal attorney	Lay term for an attorney who specializes in defending those accused of crimes. "Criminal defense attorney" is the term preferred by practitioners.
criminal law	Statutes dealing with crimes against the public. (*E.g.,* the Penal Code.)
cross-collateralization	In recording contracts, a provision which allows recoupment through withholding of additional monies from income sources other than the artist's earned royalties for a particular album. Cross-collateral may include publishing (mechanical) royalties, performance fees, or income from other projects.
cross-complainant	One who files a cross-complaint. Equivalent to "plaintiff" in a complaint.
cross-complaint	A countersuit. Complaint filed by a defendant (as cross-complainant) against a plaintiff or others, seeking relief upon particular causes of action, relating to the subject matter and occurrences underlying plaintiff's complaint. A cross-complaint is distinct from an answer, and does not relieve a defendant of the necessity of responding to plaintiff's complaint.
cross-defendant	One who is sued by a cross-complaint. Equivalent to "defendant" in a complaint.
cross-examination	The opportunity to pose questions to a witness following that witness' initial (direct) testimony.
crossover	(1) Commercial recording which obtains popular success within a *genre* (market) other than that for which it was originally intended. (2) Artist who records in a *genre* other than that for which he or she is best known.

cure provision	Contract provision which specifies what notice must given prior to claiming that a contract obligation has not been fully performed, and which allows a specified amount of time during which the other party may perform that obligation. Where a cure provision exists, the specified notice must be given, and the specified time must have elapsed without performance, in order to declare a material breach of the contract.
cue sheet	Log maintained by broadcasters, on a day by day basis, listing music played on the air, for purposes of determining royalty payments due.
culpability	Responsibility for criminal or negligent acts.
custody (1)	The holding of property under one's control.
custody (2)	(1) Incarceration. One physically held under the control of a police agency is said to be "in custody." (2) Legal and/or physical control over the person of a minor child, and responsibility for the well-being and conduct of that minor child
custody case	(1) Proceeding to determine person who shall provide primary domicile for minor child, usually arising by reason of divorce dispute over which parent shall retain custody of offspring. (2) Criminal proceeding in which the defendant remains incarcerated and is delivered daily to the court by sheriffs, marshals or bailiffs, and returned to jail after each day's proceedings.
cutout	Record company's remaining inventory of a commercial recording after production has ceased and initial retail demand has declined. Cutouts are frequently sold at (or below) cost to secondary resellers, with no (or greatly reduced) royalty to artists. Term refers to titles which have been "cut out" of the label's current order sheet and are no longer being regularly promoted for sale.

D

Δ	Greek letter "delta." Used as attorney's shorthand notation for "defendant." *Cf.*, "π" ("pi") Also used by engineers to denote a change, deviation, or vector.
damages	Court-ordered monetary compensation for loss.
DAT	Acronym for Digital Audio Tape. Computerized system which records onto magnetic tape discrete digital (numeric) data representative of the sounds recorded, rather than continuous magnetic fluctuations analogous to those sounds.
date certain	A specific date, expressly set forth in an agreement, order or judgment.
dba	Acronym for "doing business as." A fictitious business name. The term "dba" (or "d.b.a." or "d/b/a") is used following the name of the person or legal entity operating a business, and is followed by the fictitious name under which that business operates. (*E.g.,* "John Smith dba XYZ Records" or "QRS, Inc., d/b/a TUV Music.") Since a fictitious business name is not a discrete entity, any suit must be brought by or against the user of the fictitious name, who is directly liable for its business obligations. (*Cf.*, "aka," "alias," and "p/k/a.")
de facto	"In fact." A condition which may be deduced from the circumstances.
de facto **corporation**	A company which operates as though it were a corporation without first obtaining a charter or formal articles of incorporation.
de jure	"By law," as contrasted to "*de facto.*"

de minimis	Of minimal or minor importance.
de novo	Starting over. New. A trial *de novo* retries an issue as though an earlier trial or arbitration had never taken place.
deal	An agreement.
deal breaker	Condition sought by one side of negotiations which, if not accepted by the other side, will end any further negotiations.
deal memo	Short form of contract, setting forth only the most essential points of agreement with the implied or express intention that it will later be replaced by a more comprehensive "long form" contract.
deal points	The essential elements of agreement. The salient points.
debenture	Debt instrument evidencing the holder's right to receive interest and principal installments from the named obligor. Applies to all forms of unsecured, long-term debt evidenced by a certificate of debt.
debt financing	The provision of long term loans to business concerns in exchange for debt securities or a note.
debt capital	Business financing that normally requires periodic interest payments and repayment of the principal within a specified time.
debt	A monetary obligation owed by one person (the debtor) to another (the creditor)
debtor in possession	In bankruptcy reorganization (*i.e.*, Chapter 11), the term applied to the capacity under which the debtor continues to operate its business.
deceit	Acts intended to mislead or deceive; fraudulent, false, or dishonest conduct.

deception	Misleading another through intentionally false statements or concealment of facts.
decision	A judgment, decree, or determination of findings of fact and/or findings of law. A ruling by the court.
declarant	One who executes a declaration, usually signed under penalty of perjury, but not under oath. (*Cf.*, "affiant.")
declaration of mailing	A declaration attesting that a particular writing has been mailed, setting forth the date and place of mailing, and the address(es) to which has been mailed.
declaration of trust	Document signed by a settlor (trustor) creating a trust and setting forth the basic elements of its initial *corpus* (body; assets), designated trustee, and designated beneficiaries.
declaration	Statement made, usually in writing, as to certain facts which the person making the statement knows or believes to be true, generally executed under penalty of perjury.
declaratory relief	Equitable remedy in which the court makes a determination ("declaratory judgment") as to certain facts in dispute and/or as to the respective rights of the parties.
decree	Generally synonymous with judgment, a decree sets forth the court-determined rights and entitlements of the parties with respect to each other.
decriminalization	Repeal or amendment of statutes which had previously made certain acts crimes.
dedication	The giving of land by a private person or entity to the government, usually for a specified purpose such as a roadway or park.
deduction	Expenditure which taxpayer may subtract from income in calculating tax obligations.

deed of trust	A document which, when delivered, transfers a present, non-ownership interest in real property. Generally used as collateral to secure a debt. (See "Promissory Note.") Document which pledges real property to secure a loan. Also referred to as a "Trust Deed" or "TD."
deed	Written document which transfers or modifies real property ownership interest.
deem	To believe, consider, conclude, construe, determine, or hold. To treat as if .
defamation	Making of a public statement about another, orally or in print or through broadcast media, which damages that person's reputation. If the statement is untrue, and not protected as free speech, defamation is an actionable tort. (See, "libel" and "slander." See also, "public figure.")
defamatory	That which is damaging to another person's reputation.
defame	To make a public statement, orally or in print or through broadcast media, which is damaging to another person's reputation.
default judgment	Judgment entered against defendant who, after notice of suit, fails to file a timely answer or other responsive pleading.
default	Failure to timely fulfill or perform a duty or obligation.
defect	An imperfection. Defects generally fall into three categories: *(a)* "trivial" defects, which are minor or inconsequential; *(b)* "material" defects which substantially impair the function or effect of the thing affected; and *(c)* "fatal" defects, which make the thing affected completely useless, ineffective or void.
defective	Incapable of fulfilling normal function.

defendant	Party sued in a civil lawsuit or the party charged in a criminal complaint. In legal shorthand, defendant is usually abbreviated to the Greek letter Δ (delta).
defense	The effort made, and argument offered, in contradicting the allegations of a civil or criminal complaint.
deficiency judgment	Judgment for a sum greater than the value of security held.
deficit	Shortage.
defraud	Use of deceit, falsehoods, concealment or trickery to obtain money or other value from another who has detrimentally relied upon the supposed truth thereof.
delegate	To assign authority to another. One who acts with the delegated authority of another.
deleterious	Harmful; unhealthy; damaging.
deliberate	Done with care and intention or premeditation.
deliberation	Act of considering, discussing and, hopefully, reaching decision.
delinquent	Not paid in full or on time. Remiss in performance of duty or obligation.
deliver	To actually transfer custody of an object, money, document or other thing into the hands of another.
delivery	The actual handing to another of an object, money, document or other thing.
delivery provision	Contract language which specifies the time and manner in which delivery is to be made in order to be considered satisfactory.

demand	To claim as a requirement, matter of right, necessity, or entitlement.
demand note	Promissory note which is payable at any time, upon the demand of the person entitled to payment thereunder.
demise	To separate, as with one area walled off from a greater area such as commercial space leased within a larger structure.
demo	Non-commercial demonstration recording made for the purpose of promoting a composition, performer or group. A "demo" is not a "phonorecord" and its dissemination does not constitute publication for copyright purposes.
demographics	Information about a particular population or segment of population, usually grouped by age, race, education, income, or other criteria.
demography	Statistical study of populations used in conducting marketing research and polls.
demonstrative evidence	Pictures, models, actual objects, video or computer generations, or other devices which serve to demonstrate a theory and aid in understanding of that theory.
demurrer	Written response which challenges the legal effect of the pleading to which it responds. In effect, a demurrer says to the court, "Assume that every fact alleged in the complaint (or other pleading) is true, it nonetheless fails to state facts sufficient to constitute a legal action against the defendant."
denial	Responsive statement that an allegation of fact is untrue. (See also, "general denial.")
denigrate	To belittle; to insult; to reduce in stature.
deponent	Person who gives testimony at a deposition.

depose	The act of taking a deposition. Posing questions to a witness.
deposition	The taking and recording of testimony of a witness, under oath, as part of the discovery process.
depreciate	To reduce the value of an asset.
depreciation	Actual or theoretical gradual loss of value of an asset over time.
derelict	Something which has been abandoned.
dereliction	Abandonment of a possession, person or duty.
derivative action	Lawsuit brought by a corporate shareholder for the benefit of the corporation to enforce a corporate right or compel corporate action which the corporation's management has failed or refused to pursue.
derivative right	The right to control all works derived from a copyrighted work. This includes, without limitation, translations and modifications of the work. It does not protect against "fair use,"including satire or parody.
derivative work	A copyrightable work based in whole or in part on one or more previously copyrighted works. The right to control derivative works belongs exclusively to the copyright owner of the original work.
desecrate	In its literal sense, to violate the sanctity (sacred nature) of something. In copyright law, a term of art relating to compulsory licensing. There is no obligation to grant a mechanical license to a performer who intends to desecrate the original work. See "*droits morale.*"
desertion	The act of abandoning one's spouse or duty.
determinable	Capable of being determined with reasonable specificity.

detrimental reliance	Essential element of fraud. Condition of having suffered damage through believing in the supposed truth of another's misrepresentation of material fact.
devise	Archaic term for giving property by will.
devolve	When property ownership is automatically transferred from one person to another.
DHS	Acronym for Department of Homeland Security, a department of the United States government.
dicta	Plural of *dictum*. Body of legal commentary taken from within text of published opinions, distinct from the essential legal findings of such opinions.
dictum	Literally, "remark." A comment contained in a court's written opinion, but not a specific finding or conclusion of that decision. (See "*obiter dictum*.")
digital	Relating to systems which use discrete numbers to represent data. (*Cf.*, "analogue.")
Digital Millennium Copyright Act	1998 Federal Act designed to implement the 1996 World Intellectual Property Organization (WIPO) Geneva conference treaty, as well as other provisions of related copyright law. The provisions of the Act are embodied in 17 U.S.C. §§ 101, 104, 411, 507, 1201–1205. Generally abbreviated by the acronym "DMCA." (See, "DMCA" and "WIPO.")
diligence	Reasonable, prudent care and attention to a matter, usually in anticipation of a transaction. Independent verification of facts.
diminished capacity	Acting without full mental capability. Used to prove inability to form (wrongful) intent. (See "*mens rea*.")
direct evidence	Real, tangible or clear evidence of a fact, happening or event.

direct examination	The first questioning of a witness, by the party or counsel who has called that witness to testify.
direct merchandiser	Retail operation which purchases products in quantity, frequently acquiring overstock, discontinued or discounted items, and then sells directly to consumers through mail, broadcast or print advertising, or over the internet, generally at a price below normal retail, although "shipping & handling charges" may negate the discount.
directed verdict	Verdict by a jury based on a specific instruction by the judge to return that particular verdict.
director	Member of the governing board of a corporation or association.
disability	Condition which prevents one from performing all usual functions.
disbar	To permanently revoke an attorney's license to practice law.
disbarment	The act of permanently revoking an attorney's license to practice law.
disbursement	The actual payout of funds, in whole or part.
discharge	(1) to dismiss someone from a position or employment. (2) To perform one's duties and obligations.
disclaimer	Denial or renunciation of a claim, statement, intention or action. Repudiation.
discount	Arrangement by which a less-than-full payment is accepted as payment-in-full. The deducted amount under such arrangement.
discount house	Volume retail operation which purchases products in bulk and sells at a below-market retail price.

discovery	The litigation process by which the parties seek and obtain information from each other and from non-parties in order to ascertain fact and prepare for trial.
discretion	The power of a judge, public official or a private party to make a decision based upon a personal perception rather than upon some strict rule. What one <u>may</u> do (discretionary), as distinguished from what one <u>shall</u> do (non-discretionary).
discrimination	Unequal treatment of persons, for a reason not justified by facts or law.
dishonor	To refuse to perform an obligation implicit in an instrument, such as to refuse to pay out the face value of a check.
disinherit	To take such actions as will prevent a potential heir from receiving any inheritance.
diminish	To reduce in size or quantity.
dismiss	Court ruling which ends all or a portion of a case, without adjudication.
dismissal with prejudice	Dismissal which prevents a subsequent re-filing of complaint upon the same issues.
dismissal without prejudice	Dismissal which does not prevent a subsequent re-filing.
dismissal	The act of terminating all or part of a case without adjudication of issues.
disposition	Final determination by the court upon an issue.

dissent
(1) To disagree. Refuse to consent.

(2) Published opinion by one or more minority members of a reviewing court, attached as an addendum to the official opinion and setting forth legal argument for holding an opinion contrary to that of the majority opinion. A dissent may be cited as *dicta* but does not have the force of law.

dissolution of corporation
The winding down of a corporation and surrender of its corporate status.

dissolution
Divorce. The legal termination of a previously-valid marriage.

dissuade
To convince another not to proceed with a proposed course of action. To persuade someone to <u>not</u> do something which they intend to do.

distinguish
To point out fundamental differences between one case and another, and argue that a rule of law applied in one is inapplicable to the other.

distribute
The dividing of property into portions and delivery of those portions to those entitled to receive them.

distributed label
Record company which has an ongoing contract with a distributor or major label for distribution of its product. Record companies which do not have such a contract must "shop" each new album to obtain distribution.

distribution
Method by which product is conveyed from point of manufacture to point of retail sale. In the recording industry, distribution is the distinguishing factor separating major labels from all others, with the major labels having their own, direct distribution network. There are also independent distribution companies ranging from large, multinational distributors to small, regional or specialty distributors.

distributor
Entity to which manufacturers provide product, and from which retailers obtain product.

diversity of citizenship	Basis for federal jurisdiction when all defendants reside in states other than the state in which any plaintiff resides, and there is therefore said to be "complete diversity" of citizenship, invoking Article III, Section 2 of the U.S. Constitution.
divestiture	The giving up of a possession, either voluntarily or by court order. Relinquishment of ownership or control of property or interest in property.
divestment	The act of eliminating a particular property from one's holdings.
dividend	A portion of business profit paid to investors.
divorce	Termination of a valid marriage by court decree.
DMCA	Digital Millennium Copyright Act of 1998. Provides (among other things) for compulsory licensing of master recordings for digital broadcast (webcasting.) See also, "Digital Millennium Copyright Act," "webcasting" and "WIPO"
docket	(1) The various cases on file in a particular court. (2) A list of short notations indicating each pleading filed, each appearance made, and each court proceeding held or scheduled in a particular case.
doctor-patient privilege	The duty and right of a physician or therapist to refuse to testify as to any communications which occurred, or any knowledge obtained, in the course of treatment or therapy. Also, under the privilege, a patient may refuse to testify as to any information which he or she obtained through communications with the physician or therapist. Because it exists for the benefit of the patient, only the patient an elect to waive the privilege. Not available equally in all jurisdictions, it is sometimes referred to as the patient-physician privilege.
document	(1) Generic term for a paper with writing on it. (2) To memorialize an occurrence in some tangible form.

documentary evidence	A writing presented as evidence. Because a "writing" (for legal purposes) includes <u>any</u> method of preserving information, documentary evidence includes all evidence other than oral testimony, demonstrative evidence, and tangible objects which are not media of information.
Dollar One	The first income received. Royalty payments due from Dollar One are payable without being impounded for purposes of recoupment.
domestic partners	Unmarried couples, including homosexuals, living together in an arrangement generally equivalent to marriage.
domestic relations	The area of law dealing with divorce and child custody matters.
domicile	That location where a person or corporation has permanent, principal residence or principal place of business.
donor	Person or entity making a gift or donation.
door release	A general waiver of potential claims, including *droits morale*, generally coupled with permission (release) to use another's likeness in photographs. The release may be in the form of a prominently posted sign at the entry point to a studio or venue, and/or on a sign-in sheet, or (in the case of venues) printed on an admission ticket.
double jeopardy	The forbidden act of placing a person on trial a second time for an offense for which that person was previously tried and acquitted (or, if not acquittal, where jeopardy had attached during prior trial.)
doubling	Process whereby artist records additional material on top of an existing recording by that artist, to enhance or expand that prior recording. Most frequently used in reference to a lead singer adding his or her own backup vocals or harmonies through multiple recordings.

draconian	Excessively harsh, particularly in reference to penalties specified by laws or regulations.
draft	(1) *(Noun)* Less-than-final version of a document. (2) *(Noun)* Process of compelling service. (3) *(Verb)* To create a document. (4) *(Verb)* To compel another into service.
drilled	Unsold recordings which are no longer available for sale, distribution or use. When recordings were primarily on vinyl disks, an offset hole would be drilled through the unsold records to mark them as unsaleable.
droits morale	Moral rights. In entertainment and intellectual property law, *droits morale* claims generally arise in two distinct situations: (1) As rights which may be asserted by a person claiming to have made a creative contribution to a work, even without a contract. (2) As an author's right to preserve a work's artistic integrity by contesting unacceptable changes made to that work by another.
drop dead date	Colloquial term used in negotiations, or in reference to a condition embodied in a contract or a court order, which sets the last possible date by which a particular act must be performed.
dual agency	That situation which exists where two or more parties to a transaction each have the same agent, who therefor owes a fiduciary duty to them both and cannot zealously act for one at the expense of another. The agent is required to disclose such dual agency, immediately, to all affected parties. (See, "conflict of interest.")
dub	Contraction of "double." To insert a new recorded sound into an existing recording, either as an enhancement or as a replacement. Also, to record an alternative voice track for a video or film, usually in a different language from the original. See "ADR (2)"

due	Owed as of a specific date.
due and owing	A legal redundancy often seen in demands and complaints. That which is due must necessarily have been owed.
due at signing	Phrase indicating that consideration is required to be delivered concurrently with execution of contract.
due care	That prudence which a reasonable man or woman will exercise in the performance of a common act.
due course	That which occurs or is done in the normal and ordinary operation of business.
due diligence	Process of conducting a reasonable, independent investigation of facts before entering into a transaction.
due on sale	Provision requiring that some contractual obligation must be performed at the time of sale of some real or personal property. Generally seen in secured real property loans, requiring that the entire balance due becomes payable if the security is conveyed to a new owner. (See also "actually sold.")
due process	The fundamental principle establishing that fairness requires that all applicable legal rules and procedures be followed in all cases.
DUI	Acronym for "driving under the influence" of alcohol or drugs. In some jurisdictions, the charge is "driving while intoxicated," or "DWI."
duress	Physical force, imprisonment, threats of physical harm or actual physical harm against any person, used to compel that person or another to act in a manner contrary to his or her own will. Mere economic pressure or equivalent influences are not "duress" within its legal meaning.

duty   A legal obligation or responsibility, the failure to perform which can result in a claim of negligence.

duty of care   Requirement that each person act toward others and toward the public at large in a careful and conscientious manner so as to cause no harm.

DWI   Acronym for "driving while intoxicated." (See "DUI.")

dying declaration   An exception to the hearsay rule, the statement of a mortally injured person who is aware of impending death and who makes such statement about a material matter to another. A dying declaration may be introduced into evidence by the testimony of the person to whom it was made.

E

€	Currency symbol denoting "Euros."
easement	A right or privilege that a person may have on another's land, such as a right of way for ingress or egress, or to permit subterranean or overhead utility lines to pass under or over another's property.
e.g.	Abbreviation of *exempli gratia* ("free example") By way of example; for example; for instance. (*Cf.,* "i.e." "q.v." and "viz.")
ejectment	Action to remove person(s) occupying real property, without right.
election of remedy	Doctrine stating that, where two mutually-exclusive remedies exist, claimant must select one, and only one, to pursue. Particularly applicable to secured loans, where the lender may either foreclose upon the security, or file an action in contract, but not both.
electrical transcription license	See "transcription license."
eleemosynary	Not for profit; solely for charitable or altruistic purpose.
emancipation	The granting of freedom from control.
embezzlement	The crime of stealing (converting) funds or property from an employer.
embezzler	One who commits embezzlement.
emergency	Sudden, unforeseen event which requires action to correct situation, render aid, and/or to eliminate hazard arising by reason of event.

eminent domain	Power of a governmental entity to take privately-owned real property upon showing of good cause and payment of fair compensation.
emolument	Wages, salary and benefits received as compensation for employment.
emotional distress	A type of actionable damage, emotional distress can be inflicted either intentionally or negligently.
employee	Person hired for a wage, salary, fee or payment, and whose employment activities fall generally under the control of the employer.
employee at will	One who is employed without a written contract establishing a fixed term of employment. Employment-at-will may be terminated at any time, by either the employee or the employer, for any lawful reason, or for no reason at all. The employer may not, however terminate the employment for an unlawful reason. or as part of a discriminatory policy or practice. (See "wrongful termination.")
employer	Person or entity which hires the services of others to perform work for wages or salary.
employment	The hiring of a person or entity to provide services for compensation.
en banc	Literally, "in the bench," *(French)* it signifies a decision reached by the entire panel of appellate judges.
encroach	To build, erect, or place a structure, or to , plant or cultivate vegetation (trees), such that they lie in whole or in part upon the real property of another.
encroachment	A structure or vegetation which lies in whole or in part upon the property of another. Any action which utilizes another's rights, without permission.
encumbrance	Generic term for any claim or lien recorded against title to property.

endorse	(1) To publicly approve a particular position, scheme or candidate.
	(2) To sign one's name to a check or other negotiable instrument for the purpose of depositing the same or converting it into cash.
endorsement	Commercial use of an artist's name and likeness in promotion of a product which that artist ostensibly uses professionally.
endowment	Creation of a fund by gift or bequest for a particular purpose.
engineer	Person who is responsible for technical and mechanical aspects of sound enhancement in live performances (sound engineer) or for embodying such performances in a recorded, reproducible medium (recording engineer.)
enjoin	What a court does when it issue an order that someone either refrain from doing certain acts, or compelling them to perform certain acts. (See "injunction")
enjoyment	To exercise a right of use. The legal resident of a property has a right to "quiet enjoyment" of that property.
enter judgment	To officially record a judgment on the court's "judgment roll."
enterprise	A venture or undertaking, usually involving financial commitment, with related activities, unified operation, and/or common control. An enterprise can consist of a single, independent establishment or it can include subsidiaries or other branch establishments. Aggregation of all establishments owned by a parent company.
entity	Generic term for any "person," including a corporation, partnership, institution, company, or other form of recognized existence.

entrepreneur	One who assumes the financial risk of the initiation, operation and management of a given business or undertaking.
entry of judgment	The act of entering a record of judgment upon the court's docket.
environmental law	That body of law intended to protect the environment from adverse effects of human activities.
environmental impact report	A required study of all factors which a construction project of land development is likely to have upon its surroundings and the environment.
EP	Extended play. Commercial release containing three or more recordings, but fewer than a complete album.
equal protection	Right of all persons to have the same access to the law and due process.
equal opportunity	Right guaranteed by both federal and most state constitutions, seeking to provide a "level playing field" for all applicants for employment, housing, education, office or other position, without consideration of race, gender, national origin, sexual orientation or other factors deemed impermissible.
equitable lien	Lien on property in favor of someone showing a legitimate claim upon that property, although such claim may arise only by reason of justice and fair dealing, and not from a statutory basis.
equitable	Just. Based on fairness and not upon legal technicalities.
equitable estoppel	Doctrine preventing (estopping) a court from granting a judgment or other legal relief where other factors would make it unfair to do so.

Equity	In the United States, the union (Actors' Equity) which represents actors who appear in live, dramatic stage productions, as well as the stage managers and directors of such productions. In the U.K., Equity is the union in all media (stage, TV, film and radio.)
equity	(1) *(Business)* An ownership interest in a business. (2) *(Business)* Difference between value of property and debt accrued against that property. (3) *(Law)* Justice administered by court, without jury, according to principles of fairness as distinct from strict adherence to a statute or common law. Denotes actions in conformity with the spirit of justice and fairness. Actions in equity include declaratory relief and other "equitable" remedies.
equity financing	The provision of funds for capital or operating expenses in exchange for capital stock, stock purchase warrants and options in the business financed, without any guaranteed return, but with the opportunity to share in the company's profits. Equity financing includes long-term subordinated securities containing stock options and/or warrants.
equity partnership	A limited partnership arrangement for providing start-up and seed capital to businesses.
equivalent	Equal in value, force or meaning.
ergo	"Therefore." Indicating that one thing necessarily follows from another. "I've been standing in the rain, *ergo* I am wet."
err	To make a mistake; to commit error.
erroneous	In error. Wrong. Not in accordance with established law or principles.
error	Mistake in procedure or in substantive law.

errors and omissions	General term for malpractice-type insurance coverage for professionals and businesses, to cover liability which may arise by reason of negligent conduct.
escape clause	Contract provision which allows one of the parties to terminate his or her remaining obligations under the contract under certain specified conditions.
escrow	Form of account held by a neutral, third-party ("escrow agent"), charged with maintaining custody of certain instruments and funds, and delivering the same to others, all in accordance with terms and conditions of an agreement ("escrow instructions.")
escrow accounts	Funds placed in trust with a third party, for a specific purpose and to be delivered to a designated recipient only upon the fulfillment of certain conditions.
escrow agent	Person or entity holding documents and funds in a transfer account for others, and who delivers the same when certain specified conditions have been satisfied.
escrow instructions	Written instructions by which the parties to an escrow instruct the escrow agent as to what is to be received from each party, and establishing the manner and conditions upon which those things are to be distributed.
esquire	Honorific which, in the U.S., generally indicates that someone is an attorney. Usually abbreviated, "Esq." following the person's name. In ancient usage, the term referred to the assistant or apprentice of a knight.
essential elements	(1) Those factors which must be present for something to exist.
	(2) Those specific acts or occurrences which satisfy the minimum necessary to establish the basis for a cause of action (civil case) or count (criminal case). Those facts which must be alleged and proven at trial to prevail.
estate	The totality of one's assets, including all real and personal property.

estop	To halt, prevent, bar or preclude.
estoppel	A legal bar which precludes a party from a particular course or theory, based on prior events, acts, or conduct.
et al.	"And others." Abbreviation for *et alia*. Generally used in shortening the reference to parties in a case title. *E.g.*, in a case where Jones and three others, as plaintiffs, sue Smith and five others as defendants, after the initial filing the case may be referred to as <u>Jones, *et al.*, *v.* Smith, *et al*</u>
et cetera	Usually abbreviated "etc.," literally "and other things" it is used to indicate that there is more of a like or similar nature to that which precedes it. (Distinguishable from "*inter alia*" [among other (different) things] and "*et al.*" [and other (persons)].)
et seq.	"And that which follows." Abbreviation for *et sequentes*, generally used when referring to a sequence of related, numbered items, such as statutes. *E.g.*, 17 U.S.C. 501, *et seq.*
et ux.	"And wife." Abbreviated form of "*et uxor,*" found on archaic deeds and writings.
eviction	Generic term for the act of removing an occupant from residency.
evidence	Every type of proof legally presented and allowed (admitted) into evidence.
ex contractu	Arising out of a contract.
ex delicto	Arising out of a tort, crime, or malfeasance, as opposed to that which arises out of a contract ("*ex contractu.*")
ex parte	"On one side only." Generally referring to a proceeding in which only one side appears, either without notice or with minimal notice to other parties.

ex parte communication	Forbidden contact between one party or counsel and a judge, relating to the subject matter of a case pending before that judge.
ex officio	"From the office." Powers and acts which are inherently within the authority of a particular post or position, although not expressly enumerated.
ex post facto	"After the fact." Refers to something which is done or which occurs after a preceding event. Laws which seek to make illegal conduct which occurred prior to their enactment are referred to as *ex post facto* laws, and are constitutionally prohibited.
ex rel.	*Ex relatione*, meaning "upon relation or information." Legal proceedings initiated in the name of the government by attorney general or private person, referred to as the "relator."
examination	Questioning of a witness by an attorney, party, or the court.
exception (1)	That which is excused from compliance with the requirements of a particular law, rule or pattern.
exception (2)	Form of objection at trial, usually in response to the court having overruled a preceding objection, and made for the purpose of memorializing the matter for appeal. In modern practice, the exception is assumed and generally need not be stated.
exchange	To trade or barter property, goods and/or services for other property, goods and/or services.
excited utterance	Statement made in the "heat of the moment," under circumstances indicating that it was not premeditated but a true expression of the immediate thoughts and state of mind of the speaker. Such statements fall within an exception to the hearsay rule.

exclusionary rule   Law which provides that evidence secured by illegal means or in bad faith, and all other evidence derived from it, will not be admitted into evidence at trial.

exclusive   That which excludes others. *E.g.*, an exclusive contract requires that the bound party not provide similar goods or services to anyone else during the contract term

exclusivity clause   Contract provision which prohibits a party from entering into contracts with others during the term of the exclusive contract. *E.g.* an exclusive recording contract prevents the artist from recording for anyone else during its term.

exculpatory   That which tends to exonerate or excuse the conduct of one accused of wrongful acts.

excusable neglect   Legitimate excuse for failure of a party or counsel to timely perform a duty. Grounds for setting aside a default.

execute   (1) To finish, complete or perform as required, as in fulfilling one's contractual obligation. (2) To sign a document. (3) To carry out a court order or judgment.

executive order   Decree by the President or a Governor which has the force of law.

executor   Person appointed to administer an estate.

executory   Something required (as by contract) but not yet performed or done.

exemplar   A sample or example, usually of handwriting, signature, or other personally identifiable trait, used for comparison to verify or challenge authenticity of a writing.

exemplary damages	Damages which may be sought and awarded against a defendant in a civil action for wrongful conduct. Generally only awarded after proof that the conduct complained of was wanton, willful, malicious, oppressive, outrageous, and/or shocking to the conscience. Exemplary damages are effectively identical to "punitive" damages, differing only in the rationale underlying their imposition, the rationale for exemplary damages being that they are awarded for the purpose of discouraging the defendant *and others* from engaging in such conduct in future. (See also, "punitive damages")
exhibit	A document or object (*e.g.,* a photograph) produced in court or attached to a pleading or other writing, and generally marked and referred to by a letter or number (*e.g.* "Exhibit A," or "Exhibit 1.") An exhibit may be <u>offered</u> as evidence, but it does not <u>become</u> evidence until admitted by the Court as such.
exhibition copy	Copy of an audiovisual work which is intended solely for non-home viewing, such as for television broadcast, for projection in a commercial movie theater, or as an in-flight movie, or for use in a video jukebox.
expedite	To perform quickly. To hasten. In business, the term is frequently used in regard to completion of projects, or processing and shipping orders, to such extent that it is sometimes used as a synonym of "to process" or "to ship."
expert testimony	Opinions stated during trial or deposition by a person having specialized knowledge which may be helpful to the court or jury in understanding an issue within the scope of that knowledge. (*E.g.,* in a shooting case, an expert on ballistics may be hired to testify.)
expert witness	A specialist in a subject who, usually for a fee, testifies as to his opinion within the area of his or her specialty.

exploit	To make use of. In common usage, "exploit" has a negative connotation. In the entertainment industry, however, it refers to placement of products and product-related merchandise in various markets for the purpose of maximizing revenue.
exploitation	Act of placing or exposing product in various markets.
express	Actually stated in direct, unambiguous, distinct language.
express contract	Contract in which all elements are specifically stated in a manner which is not reasonably subject to inconsistent interpretations.
expropriation	The taking of property or rights by a superior authority.
extension	A specific amount of extra time granted by another to perform some task or obligation.
extenuating circumstances	Surrounding factors which may be taken into account in determining culpability of conduct. (*E.g.*, an extenuating circumstance of threat may convert the crime of homicide into the non-crime of "justifiable homicide.") See "mitigation"
extinguish	To cancel or destroy a right.
extinguishment	Cancellation or destruction of a right.
expenses	Total of money expended, including all costs and overhead.
extortion	Obtaining money or property by threat to a victim's property, person, reputation, family or associates. (See "blackmail.")
extradition	Surrender by one state or country to another of a person charged with crime in that other state or country.

extrajudicial

Referring to actions outside the judicial system, whether legal or illegal. "Extrajudicial" may refer to mediation (legal) or to lynching (illegal.)

extrinsic fraud

Fraudulent acts conducted in the course of legal proceedings, but not within the scope of the matters at issue in those proceedings. *(E.g.,* Obtaining a default judgment by falsely representing that a defendant has been served)

F

f	Currency symbol for "francs."
fact	That which has actually occurred. An actual thing or occurrence. Material facts are those which must be proven at trial to establish each of the essential elements of a cause of action or of a particular crime charged. Facts are to be distinguished from opinions, interpretations, theories, arguments, speculations, and conclusions.
factoring	Type of prearranged financing in which the lender (factor) pays the seller a discounted percentage of accounts receivable when they are invoiced, and the full amount of those invoices becomes directly payable to the factor rather then the seller.
failure of consideration	Not delivering goods or services promised in a contract. Grounds for breach or rescission of contract.
fair market value	The amount for which property, goods or services could be obtained on the open market. Generally abbreviated, "FMV."
fair use	The protected privilege to use copyrighted material in a reasonable manner without the express consent of the copyright owner.
false arrest	Physical detention of someone from further movement, without a legal right to do so.
false imprisonment	The physical holding a person in detention without legal right to do so.
federal question	A basis for filing a lawsuit in federal district court (rather than state court), on the ground that the lawsuit states a cause of action under a specific federal law.

fee (1)	Sum of money or other thing of value paid to another for services rendered.
fee (2)	Title to land. To hold land "in fee" or "in fee simple," is to own it free of any competing ownership by another.
felon	Person who has been convicted of a felony.
felonious	Referring to an act done with criminal intent.
felony	Crime sufficiently serious to be punishable by imprisonment for more than 1 year, or by death.
fictitious defendants	Persons whose names may be unknown to plaintiff, but who are nonetheless included within the lawsuit under convenient designations such as "DOE 1 through 10," with the plaintiff reserving the right to substitute their true names when they have been discovered.
fidelity	Faithfulness. Quality of being true, honest, trustworthy, and loyal. (See "fiduciary.")
fidelity bond	A type of insurance which may be purchased to cover losses through embezzlement or similar misconduct by a trusted employee or fiduciary. Generally, the insurer will investigate the character and background of a proposed fiduciary before agreeing to issue a fidelity bond. Fidelity bonds are often considered in connection with management contracts, particularly where the manager holds a power of attorney.
fiduciary	Person holding a position of, or analogous to, a trustee, having a duty to another to exercise the highest standards of trustworthiness, candor, and scrupulous good faith.
fiduciary relationship	That relationship which exists where one person (the principal) is entitled to repose complete confidence and trust in another (the fiduciary.) (*E.g.*, the relationship between a depositor and a bank; or between a client and attorney.)

file	To deposit a document with the clerk of the court for entry on the docket of that case, either to initiate a new lawsuit or as part of an action previously filed. (See also, "lodged.")
final decree	Final judgment in cases for declaratory relief, or in jurisdictions using the word "decree" in lieu of "judgment."
final judgment	Written determination by the judge who presided of the final outcome of a lawsuit.
financing	Money obtained from sources other than regular income. *E.g.,* from outside investment (equity financing) or through borrowing (debt financing).
finder of fact	The person or persons with authority to decide which facts have been sufficiently proven, according to a given standard of proof. In proceedings where there is both a judge and a jury, it is the jury which is the finder of fact. Absent a jury, it is the judge or other official(s) conducting the proceedings.
finding	Determination of a factual question relevant to a lawsuit.
findings of fact	Written statement, usually prepared by counsel and signed by the judge who presided, setting forth the court's conclusions regarding particular factual questions.
first impression	A legal issue which has never been previously decided, or as to which there is no prior published opinion by a court of equivalent jurisdiction.
first refusal	A contractual agreement which obligates one party to offer the other party an opportunity to purchase a property prior to offering that property to anyone else, or an opportunity to match an offer made by a third party for that property.

first sale	Doctrine which provides that royalties are only earned on the first sale of each copy of a copyrighted work, and that subsequent leasing or sale of that particular copy will not give rise to additional royalties
first use	In copyright law, the exclusive right of the creator of a work to control the first publication, release, or other initial use of that work.
fiscal	Referring to finance.
fiscal year	Twelve month accounting period which may be arbitrarily set to begin on any day of the calendar year. *E.g.,* a business' fiscal year may be October 1 through September 30 of each year.
fixture	A structure, piece of equipment, or other item which has been attached to real estate and cannot be readily removed.
FMV	See "Fair Market Value"
FOB	Acronym for "free on board," the term is invariably followed by the name of a locale (*E.g,* "FOB New York, NY" or "FOB Delivered") and is used in commercial law to designate the geographical point at which control of shipped goods is deemed to have been transferred from one party to another. The location to which the seller has agreed to deliver such goods as part of the selling price.
for value received	Phrase used in some contracts, acknowledging delivery and acceptance of consideration.
forbearance	Intentional delay in collecting a debt or demanding performance of an obligation, usually at the request of the obligated party.
force majeure	A superior or irresistible force. In contract law, the term is used to allow for unforeseeable events of such impact that they excuse or prevent a party from fully performing obligations otherwise required.

forced sale	Sale of goods seized by sheriff to satisfy an outstanding judgment debt.
forcible entry	Crime (and tort) of taking possession of a house or other structure by either breaking in, or through force or threats.
foreclosure sale	Forced sale of property at a public auction.
foreclosure	Action by which one who has lent money secured by specific property may cause that property to be sold to satisfy the outstanding obligation. Foreclosure may be non-judicial (based on specific contract terms alone) or judicial (court-ordered, based upon contract or on other legal or equitable principles.)
foreign corporation	Corporation which is incorporated under the laws of a different state or country.
forensic	Literally, "belonging to the court," the term has come to refer to anything relating to, used in, or appropriate for, courts, public discussions, or debate. (*E.g.* a "forensic accountant" is an expert witness who testifies as to accounting matters at trial.)
forensics	Debate or public speaking.
foreseeability	That anticipation which a reasonable person is presumed to have of the possible or likely results of an action.
forfeit	To lose property or rights involuntarily as a penalty for some error, fault, neglect of duty, offense, or crime.
forfeiture	A loss of property due to violation of law.
forgery	Crime of creating a false document or altering a document.
forthwith	Immediately. At once. Without delay.

Form CA	Copyright form used to modify a previous filing or registration, such as to change ownership of a copyright.
Form CON	Copyright form used as an attachment to registration forms, to provide for additional information for which there is no room on the primary form.
Form PA	Copyright form for registration of creative works which are meant to be performed, such as musical compositions, song lyrics (as distinct from poetry), plays, screenplays, and other works of Performing Art.
Form SR	Copyright form for registration of Sound Recordings.
Form TX	Copyright form for registration of literary works not meant to be performed, including books, stories, liner notes, poems (as distinct from "lyrics"), or other textual works.
Form VA	Copyright form for registration of works of Visual Art, including photographs, artwork, sketches, creative designs, and other visual presentations. An album cover may be copyrighted using Form VA.
formalities	Legal necessities, even if only for the sake of form or ceremony. Generally used in connection with procedural requirements, such as conducting annual shareholders' meetings, keeping corporate minutes books current, filing annual statements of officers, and similar requirements. A failure to comply with required formalities may provide *indicia* of lack of separate existence of a corporate entity. (See "alter ego" and "pierce the corporate veil.")
forum	The place in which a dispute is resolved, whether a court of law, tribunal, arbitration, mediation or other such place.

foundation	Preliminary questions to a witness to establish authenticity of evidence so as to permit it to be introduced. "Lacks foundation" is an objection calling for exclusion of evidence which cannot be properly authenticated by such testimony. See "chain of custody." *Cf.*, "exceptions to hearsay rule."
four corners	Term used to describe those elements which appear within the body of a writing, as distinct from what may be inferred.
fourwall	To take over a venue entirely, by contract, for the purpose of producing a concert or other presentation. Under a fourwall agreement, the landlord usually receives a fixed sum as rent plus a percentage of revenues, while the producer or promoter is responsible for staffing, maintaining and operating the venue during the term of the agreement. The practice is generally referred to as "fourwalling."
franchise (1)	A special privilege conferred by government or other regulatory body which does not belong to all citizens as a matter of right. (*E.g.*, the "right" to vote or to register a trademark are matters of franchise.)
franchise (2)	In business, a continuing relationship in which the franchisor provides a licensed privilege to the franchisee to do business, and offers assistance in organizing, training, merchandising, marketing and managing in return for a consideration. Franchising is a form of business by which the owner (franchisor) of a product, service or method obtains distribution through affiliated dealers (franchisees). The product, method or service being marketed is usually identified by the franchisor's brand name, and the holder of the privilege (franchisee) is often given exclusive access to a defined geographical area.
franchise tax	State tax on individuals or businesses.
fraud	Intentional use of deceit, a trick or some dishonest practice to induce another to act in reliance thereon to their detriment.

fraud in the inducement	Use of deceit or trick to cause someone to act to his or her detriment in entering into some agreement or performing some other act. Grounds for rescission of contract.
fraudulent conveyance	Transfer of title to property to another for the purpose of concealing assets or to place them outside the immediate reach of creditors.
free agent	One who is at liberty to contract with anyone. One who is not under any contractual prohibition against contracting with others.
free goods	Saleable merchandise delivered by record companies to retailers, ostensibly without charge. Since recording contracts generally provide that royalties are only paid for albums which are "sold," the artist receives nothing for these "free goods," which are really no more than a normal trade discount to volume retailers. See "actually sold" and "creative accounting."
freedom	Liberty. The absolute right do as one pleases, limited only by restrictions imposed by law and public policy.
Freedom of Information Act	Federal statute (5 USC § 552) which requires the government to make available to members of the public, on request, certain types of public (government) records which are not generally published or available for public viewing. Although there are documents which are not available under the Act because of national security or other similar reasons, denial of a request is subject to appeal and review. The intention of the Act is to prevent abuse of government power through suppression of internal memoranda and work product.
freehold	Ownership of real property, in fee, or a right to possession and use of such real property for life.
frivolous	Referring to a lawsuit, or tactics adopted within such suit, which are not intended for their apparent purpose, but rather to vex, annoy, or harass the other party, or to delay proceedings.

fruit of the poisonous tree	In criminal law, the doctrine that evidence discovered illegally, and all evidence subsequently discovered which would not certainly have been discovered without the illegally obtained evidence, is tainted and cannot be introduced or referred to at trial.
FSO	Acronym for "furnishing [the] services of," used to refer to the individual artist, producer, or other person whose services are being provided through a loan-out agreement with a third party, such as a corporation.. (See "loan out" and "side letter.")
full faith and credit	Article IV, Section 1 of the United States Constitution requiring each state to accept acts of each other state as proper and lawful.
full disclosure	Requirement that parties to business transactions tell the "whole truth" to each other.
fungible	Those items of property which are completely interchangeable, with each unit thereof being identical in nature and value to any other equal unit. (*E.g.*., a gallon of crude oil is deemed equivalent to any other gallon of crude oil.) Fungible property may be readily distinguished from non-fungible property (*e.g.*, real property, intellectual property) by comparison of one unit to another. If there are unique, material characteristics, the property is not fungible. *E.g.*, two copies of the same edition of the same book, by the same author, in the same binding, neither of which has been altered by annotation, may be fungible; a first edition and a recent paperback copy of that same book are not..
future interest	An interest in real or personal property which will come into being at some time in the future. (*E.g.*, an advance due upon delivery of a completed album is a future interest prior to that delivery.)

G

GAAP Acronym for "Generally Accepted Accounting Principles." Accounting methods, standards and practices which are commonly used and deemed acceptable throughout the accounting profession

GAAS Acronym for "Generally Accepted Auditing Standards." Accounting standards and practices which are commonly used and deemed acceptable by independent auditors.

gag order Court order prohibiting the attorneys, parties and/or others subject to the court's jurisdiction from publicly discussing or commenting upon a particular case or issue.

gamut The entire range or scope of something. Contraction of gamma-ut *(Medieval Latin)* derived from *gamma* (third letter of the Greek alphabet) used to represent the lowest musical tone on the scale, plus *ut*, which denoted the highest note on that scale. The medieval scale was derived from the initial syllables of a Latin hymn; *ut, re, mi, fa, sol, la, si. Ut* and *si* later became the now familiar *do* and *ti.*

gaol Archaic spelling of "jail," still used in some areas.

garnish To obtain payment of debt by court order directing holder of monies owing to debtor to instead pay all or a portion of such money to a court officer for the benefit of the person obtaining the court order.

garnishment Process of petitioning for and obtaining a court order allowing interception and collection of funds otherwise payable to debtor. (*E.g.,* garnishment of wages.)

general appearance	First appearance in court by a party or party's counsel, unless such appearance is for the purpose of challenging jurisdiction. Once a party (or counsel for that party) has "generally appeared," that party is completely subject to that court's *in personam* jurisdiction for the duration of the case.
general counsel	Regular attorney for a corporation or other entity, usually receiving a regular retainer or, in some instances, a salary as an employee or officer of the company.
general damages	Sum of money awarded in a lawsuit for injuries actually suffered.
general denial	Permissible response made by a defendant in answer to a lawsuit or claim, in which everything alleged is "generally denied" without specifically admitting or denying any particular allegation.
general partner	In a general partnership, each of the partners. In a limited partnership, the partner(s) actively involved in management of the business. General partners are personally liable for the obligations of the business in which they are partners.
genre	Literally "type" or "kind." *(French)*. A style or category of artistic composition, marked by a distinctive form, content, or intended audience.
germane	Relevant; pertinent; applicable.
ghost writer	An author or composer who performs creative services for hire, allowing another's name to be published as being the creator of the work, instead of his or her own.

golden parachute	Provision in employment contract which provides for substantial benefits to employee in the event of early termination or changes within the employer's business structure. Generally, such provisions are found only in contracts of the most senior corporate executives, and are intended, in part, to discourage corporate takeovers which would trigger those provisions. (See also "poison pill.")
good cause	Legally sufficient reason for a judicial ruling, finding, or other action.
good faith	Honest intent to act without taking unfair advantage. In every contract there is an implied covenant that the parties are acting in good faith with respect to each other.
good title	Ownership of real property which is totally free of adverse claims.
goods	Items held for sale in the regular course of business.
goodwill	An intangible asset of a business, based on its good reputation and existing relationships.
governmental immunity	Doctrine providing that governmental employees cannot be sued personally for actions performed within the regular course and scope of their official duties.
grace period	Time stated in a contract during which late performance of an obligation will not be deemed delinquent or made cause for penalties or claim of breach. (See, "cure provision.")
grand jury	A jury which serves for a protracted term, or for a special purpose, empaneled to determine if there is sufficient grounds for criminal prosecution. (See "indictment."; see also "jury.")
grand larceny	Crime of theft of another's property (including money) having a value in excess of a certain, statutory sum (*e.g.*, $400.)

grand right	Performance right in dramatic work of musical composition.
grand theft	See "grand larceny."
grandfather clause	An exception included in some regulations which permits those already engaged in a newly-proscribed (but previously permitted) activity to continue in that activity.
grant	To transfer real property from a title holder (grantor) to a new title holder (grantee.)
grant deed	Document which transfers title to real property, with warranty of good title. (*Cf.* "Quitclaim.")
grantee	Person who receives title to real property by grant deed.
grantor	Person who transfers title to real property to another by grant deed.
gratuitous	Voluntary or free. Done without consideration.
gravamen	Literally, "to weigh down" *(Latin)* The basic claims asserted by a legal action.
gross income	Total income before deductions or credits.
gross negligence	Violation of a duty owed, in reckless disregard for the safety of others.
guarantee	To pledge or agree to be responsible for another's debt.
guarantor	Person who agrees to be responsible for another's debt.
guaranty	See "guarantee."
guardian	Person who has been appointed to take care of a minor.

guardian *ad litem*   Person appointed by the court only to take legal action for and on behalf of a minor.

guild   Association of individuals with common profession, vocation, craft, or trade.   A union.

guilty   A plea admitting having committed a crime. Verdict convicting one of having committed a crime.

H

habeas corpus

Literally, "you have the body." *(Latin)* Proceeding to compel a judicial determination as to the legal sufficiency of due process. The right to *habeas corpus* was considered so essential that it is the only specific individual right included within the body of the Constitution, rather than within the subsequent Bill of Rights (Amendments I through X.)

harass

To systematically and/or continually annoy, alarm, or vex another by words, gestures, or other intentional conduct.

harassment

The act of harassing another.

harmless error

Error by the court which had no appreciable effect on the outcome of the matter being considered. (*Cf.*, "clear error.")

Harry Fox Agency

Licensing agency for U.S. music publishers founded in 1927 by the National Music Publisher's Association as an information source, clearinghouse and monitoring service for licensing musical copyrights. The agency issues mechanical licenses, collects and distributes mechanical royalties, and pursues piracy claims on behalf of its clients.

headnote

A summary of a key legal point extracted from an opinion, headnotes are generally found preceding the opinion from which they are taken, or as annotations to statutes to which they are relevant.

hearing

Any proceeding before a judge, magistrate, or other official.

hearsay

Second-hand evidence in which the witness is reporting what he or she has been told by another, or has read, rather than speaking as to matters of personal knowledge.

hearsay rule Basic rule of evidence stating that testimony or documents which quote other sources are not generally admissible, with certain well-established exceptions.

hearsay exceptions Certain records, statements and actions which might otherwise be considered hearsay, are nonetheless admissible into evidence under well-settled exceptions to the hearsay rule which include, but are not limited to, the following:

Admission Against Interest; testimony as to a prior statement in which a party has admitted to facts which are contrary to that party's interests.

Ancient Writings; documents of certain age (*e.g.,* 30 years) are deemed admissible.

Adoption - Tacit Admission; testimony as to conduct by a party in which that party failed to refute an accusation, or appeared to accept a statement as being true.

Authorized Statement; evidence of a statement made by a party's authorized representative.

Business Records; documentary evidence of normal and customary business records.

Confession; testimony as to a party's admission of guilt.

Dying Declaration; statement made by ill or injured person while in expectation of imminent death.

Excited Utterance - Spontaneous Declaration; testimony about a party's statement made in the heat of the moment.

Learned Treatise; written work of scholarly nature generally accepted as authoritative in its field.

Official Records; certified records of governmental agencies or bodies, or of court proceedings.

Prior Inconsistent Statement; testimony regarding a declarant's statements which are contradictory to that party's current testimony or argument.

Statements of Physical or Mental State; testimony as to a party's statements regarding that party's physical condition or state of mind.

heir	One who acquires property upon the death of another, either by the terms of the deceased's will, or on the basis of a blood or adoptive relationship to the deceased.
held	Decided or ruled. Judicial determination of an issue.
hence	This short, useful, Old English word has multiple meanings.
	(1) For this reason; therefore. (*E.g.,* Never disciplined as a child, hence irresponsible as an adult.)
	(2) From this source. (*E.g.,* Shakespeare coined several new words which we now take for granted. Hence "articulate" and "forced." among others.)
	(3) From this time. (*E.g.,* Return a year hence.)
	(4) From this place. (*E.g.,* You shall be taken hence to a place of confinement.)
	(*Cf.,* "thence" and "whence.")
henceforth	From this moment forward in time. From now on. (See also, "thenceforth")
hereditament	Any kind of property which can be inherited.
herein	Within this document; within these proceedings.
hereinabove	At some earlier point in this particular document.
hereinafter	From this point forward. Generally used in contracts to denote a defined term. *E.g.,* "John Doe (hereinafter 'Artist')."
hereinbelow	At some later point in this particular document. Generally used to indicate that related or referenced information may be found further along in the same writing. Usually, but not always, a page or paragraph number will be indicated to clarify where the information is to be found.
heretofore	Before now; up until now. Formerly. *E.g.,* "The artist heretofore known as Prince."

hidden asset	Item of value which does not show on the books of a business.
highest and best use	Method used for determining value of property based on its most valuable potential use rather than its current use.
hobby loss	In tax law, a nondeductible loss from an activity engaged in for purposes other than profit. A business which does not occasionally show profit may be redefined as a "hobby," thereby eliminating the deductibility of its costs and expenses, resulting in substantial tax liability.
hold harmless	Promise to pay any costs or claims which may accrue against the person to whom the promise has been made.
holder in due course	One holding a check or promissory note, received for value given in the ordinary course of business, in good faith and without knowledge that it has been dishonored, is overdue, or is subject to adverse claims.
holding	Any ruling or decision of a court.
holding company	A company, usually a corporation or LLC, which is created for the purpose of owning property, including other businesses, but not itself providing any goods or services.
holdover tenancy	Capacity of tenant of real property who continues to occupy that property after expiration of the term of lease or rental agreement, usually on a month-to-month basis.
holographic will	A will, dated, signed by, and entirely in the handwriting of, the testator.
homestead	House and property occupied by the owner as the head or the household, as a primary residence. On a state-by-state basis, homesteads are protected from collection actions by creditors, usually up to some monetary limit.

homicide	Killing of a human by the act or omission of another, purposely, knowingly, recklessly, or negligently.
honorarium	A payment made for professional services.
hook	Musical phrase within a song which is particularly unique, memorable, compelling or appealing.
hornbook law	A fundamental and well-accepted legal principle. A hornbook is a primer, setting forth basic fundamentals.
hostile witness	A witness who is on the adverse side of a case, or who the court finds has demonstrated an attitude of evasiveness or animosity with respect to the questioning party. Hostile witnesses may be questioned by the use of leading questions not otherwise permitted.
hot pursuit	Doctrine which permits a police agency which is pursuing closely behind a suspect, in an attempt to apprehend, to cross jurisdictional boundaries.
house counsel	An attorney who works exclusively (or primarily) for a particular business or who maintains his offices within that business' premises and is therefore readily available to that business; also referred to as "in-house counsel."
household	A family, living together.
hung jury	A jury so irreconcilably divided in opinion as to be unable to agree upon a verdict.
hypothecate	Generic term for using property as collateral. Property which has been encumbered as collateral is said to have been "hypothecated."

1

i.e.   Abbreviation for *id est (Latin)* meaning "that is," "*i.e.*" is used to denote a specific matter to which a preceding statement definitely refers, rather than merely an example to which it might refer. (*Cf.*, "e.g." and "viz.")

I-9   INS/DHS form which all employers are required to complete for each employee, regardless of the employee's nationality or citizenship. The form must be retained throughout employment and for at least three years thereafter, but need not be filed.

I-129   INS/DHS form required to obtain a work visa for a non-citizen to legally enter the U.S. The formal title of the form is "Petition for a Nonimmigrant Worker." Since artist's services are unique, the petition is generally approved as a matter of routine for recording artists and other performers, unless they have a history which is deemed to pose questions of national security.

IFPI   Acronym for "International Federation of Phonographic Industries," a recording and music-video industry trade association based in London (with regional offices in Brussels, Hong Kong, Miami, and Moscow) engaged in promoting the music industry and combating piracy.

illegal   That which is in violation of a statute, regulation or ordinance. Contrary to some specific law.

illusory promise   A promise that actually promises nothing because it is so indefinite that it leaves the promissor free to either perform or not perform, or with an alternative which, if taken, gives the promisee nothing.

immaterial   That which is not pertinent or essential to the matter at hand; irrelevant.

immediate	(1) At once and without delay. (2) Directly proximate, as in "immediate family."
imminent	Immediate. Impending.
imminent domain	Legal process by which governmental agency may compel the sell of private property for a price set through legal determination by proving that some public purpose would be served as a result.
imminent harm	Immediate peril. Grounds for obtaining a temporary restraining order to prevent or abate condition or conduct posing risk of such harm.
immunity	Exemption from penalties, payments or legal requirements.
impanel	To select and install a jury.
impeach	To discredit the testimony of a witness by proving that his testimony is either contrary to prior statements made by that same witness, or demonstrably false by reason of facts which may be judicially noticed.
impeachment	The act of discrediting (impeaching) a witness.
impinge	To encroach or overlap.
impleader	A procedural device before trial in which a new party is brought into an action already commenced by other parties.
implied	That which can be deuced from circumstances, conduct, or statements, as distinct from that which is specifically stated.
implied consent	When conduct and surrounding circumstances exist which would tend to indicate that consent had been given, as by acquiescence (silence), or by subsequent ratification.

implied contract	An agreement which is found to exist based on the circumstances and the conduct of the parties, although they never reduced the terms of their agreement to specific words.
implied covenant	A promise which is imputed to a contract, although not specifically expressed in words within that contract. See "good faith."
implied warranty	Legal assumption that products are "merchantable," meaning that they are provided in good order and suitable for the purpose for which they are marketed.
impossibility	An act which cannot be performed due to nature, physical impediments, or other material conditions which prevent performance, and which were not caused intentionally or negligently by the person obligated to perform.
impound	To collect and hold funds of another for a specific purpose.
improvement	Any permanent structure on real property, or any work performed in regard to the property, beyond mere repair or maintenance, intended to enhance the property's value
impute	To attach to a person certain knowledge, legal responsibility and/or financial liability, for the acts or knowledge of another over whom the person has control or for whose acts or knowledge the person is legally responsible.
in absentia	Literally, "in absence" *(Latin)*, referring to proceedings conducted in the absence of a party over whom the Court nonetheless has proper jurisdiction. *E.g.*, a criminal defendant who flees the court's jurisdiction (*i.e.*, absconds) before verdict or sentencing, may nonetheless be sentenced *in absentia*.

in camera	Literally, "in chambers." *(Latin)* Refers to proceedings which are conducted in private, usually in the judge's chambers and generally for the purpose of considering admissibility of matters which one party seeks to be kept secret for good cause. (*E.g.*, the Court may conduct an *in camera* inspection of documents which one party claims to contain "trade secrets," to determine if they must be produced in evidence, or if they can be redacted (edited) to eliminate legitimately secret material.)
in chambers	Discussions, conferences or hearings held in the judge's chambers, rather than in open court.
in extremis	In extreme distress; extremely ill or potentially dying.
in fee simple	Manner in which one holds clear title to real property.
in forma pauperis	Literally, "in the manner (form) of a pauper." *(Latin)* A procedure whereby a person unable to pay court fees and costs may nonetheless be permitted to file and prosecute, or to defend against, a lawsuit by obtaining a court order waiving or deferring court fees and costs.
in haec verba	Literally, "in these words" *(Latin)* or "in the same words." Identical utterances or writings.
in kind	Payment, distribution or substitution of things which are of a common nature. *I.e.*, exchanging cash for cash, real property for real property, *etc.* See also, "fungible."
in lieu	Instead. In the place of something else.
in limine	Literally, "at the threshold." *(Latin)* Refers to matters which are heard just before trial commences, usually motions to exclude or limit the introduction at trial of certain matters, evidence, testimony, or lines of questioning.
in loco parentis	Literally, "in the place of a parent." *(Latin)* Refers to a person who is temporarily vested with a parent's rights, duties and responsibilities in respect to a minor child.

in or around	Phrase referring to a month, year, or locale which is approximate. Also written, "in or about." (See also "at or around" and "on or around")
in pari delicto	Literally, "in equal fault" *(Latin)*, refers to one who is equally culpable or criminal with another.
in perpetuity	Of endless duration; forever.
in personam	Literally, "against (directed toward) the person" *(Latin)*, refers to matters where the acts of a particular person are at issue. Once a person has been served in a lawsuit, the court is said to have *in personam* jurisdiction over that person.
in pro per	Abbreviated form of *"in propria persona"* (*Latin;* "in one's proper person") Designation applied in some jurisdictions to a natural person who appears on his or her own behalf, without an attorney. See also, *"pro se."*
in propria persona	See *"in pro per."*
in re	In the matter of; concerning; regarding. Generally used in cases where there are not adverse parties, but rather a single party or thing which is the subject matter of the case. Thus, a bankruptcy case is referred to as *In re* [Debtor's name].
in rem	Literally, "against (directed toward) a thing." *(Latin)* Designates proceedings or actions brought against a thing, as defendant, rather than against a person. In an action where the Court acquires control over a thing which is a subject matter of the case, the Court is said to exercise *in rem* jurisdiction over that thing.
in terrorem **clause**	A contract or will provision designed to frighten a person into doing or not doing some particular thing. *E.g.,* in a will, a provision which disinherits an heir who contests the will. (See also, "poison pill.")
in toto	Literally, "in total." *(Latin)* Denotes the whole of a thing. Completely; entirely.

inadmissible evidence	Proffered evidence which is held by the court to be unacceptable for consideration by the trier of fact.
inapposite	Not applicable. Not pertinent, germane or suitable. Distinguishable from the matter under consideration.
incapacity	An inability to perform.
incept license	Negotiated mechanical license given by copyright owner for the first-ever recording or use of a composition. There is no standard or statutory rate for such a license. (See "first use" and "mechanical license.")
inchoate	Referring to something which has begun but has not yet been completed. *E.g.*, a contract which has been signed by some but not yet all of the necessary parties is an inchoate agreement.
incidental	Depending upon or pertaining to something else which is primary. Something which necessarily follows from some principal action or provision.
incidentals	Miscellaneous items of expense.
income	Money, goods or other economic benefit received. Revenue.
income statement	A financial report, summarizing the income, expenditures and resulting profit of a business or project over a specified period of time. Also referred to as a "profit and loss statement" or "P/L.")
incompatibility	Condition in which two or more persons or things cannot comfortably coexist in proximity to each other.
incompatible	Inconsistent, non-matching, mutually exclusive.
incompetency	Condition of lacking the legal capacity or actual ability to handle one's affairs.

incompetent	One who lacks legal capacity or actual ability to manage his/her/its affairs.
incompetent evidence	Testimony, documents or things which are held to be inadmissible under applicable rules of evidence, as distinct from "excluded" evidence which is not admitted for reasons extrinsic to the probative value of the evidence itself.
incontrovertible evidence	Evidence which is so compelling in proving a particular fact, that there is no possibility of other evidence which would disprove that fact. *E.g.,* an official, certified copy of articles of incorporation from the files of the Secretary of State is incontrovertible evidence of the fact that articles of incorporation had been filed.
incorporate	(1) To include one thing into another. (2) To form a corporation.
incorporate by reference	To include language from another document or elsewhere into a document or pleading, by identifying that other writing in the new document and stating that it is being incorporated by that reference.
incorporation	The act of incorporating an organization, *i.e.,* forming a corporation.
incorporeal	That which is not physically tangible.
incriminate	To make a statement that expressly or impliedly indicates that oneself or another has participated in the commission of a crime.
incumbrance	Generic term for any obligation which attaches to property, as collateral securing that obligation, such that the property cannot be conveyed without acknowledgment of that obligation.
indefeasible	That which cannot be altered, revoked or voided, usually applied to an estate or right which cannot be successfully challenged.

indemnify	To promise another to pay for losses which that other might suffer, usually including a duty to defend and to reimburse all costs and expenses incurred. (See "hold harmless")
indemnity	A legal device for shifting ultimate liability from one person to another. A contract of assurance by which one party agrees to secure another against an anticipated loss or action, or to prevent the indemnified party from the legal and/or financial consequences of an act or forbearance to act. Indemnity can be established by statute, contract, or by a proceeding in equity.
indemnity provision	Contract language which provides that one party will indemnify the other in the event of third-party claims or for costs and expenses resulting from the indemnifying party's non-performance of contract obligations. (See also, "warranties and representations.")
independent	A record or production company which operates on a smaller scale, usually without an ongoing distribution agreement.
independent contractor	A person or business which performs services for another, without being an employee of that other. The distinguishing ark of an independent contractor (as compared to an employee), is that the independent contractor is truly "independent," whereas an employee is under the control of the employer as to when, where and how work is to be performed. Generally, and independent contract will perform similar services, as a regular business, for a number of other businesses, will have a business licence, a tax identification number, and other *indicia* of independent business operation.
indeterminate sentence	Prison term imposed which is for the maximum time authorized by law, but which is subject to reduction by a parole board or other agency at any time after a minimum portion of the sentence has been served.

indicia	Literally, "signs." *(Latin)* Refers to matters from which other matters can be logically inferred. Facts which indicate some other fact.
indictment	Charge of a felony (serious crime) issued upon the vote of a Grand Jury.
indigent	Person so poor that he or she cannot provide for the basic necessities of life.
indispensable party	Person or entity who or which must be included in a lawsuit so that the matter can be fairly adjudicated. (See "necessary party."
indorse	Act of executing an endorsement.
indorsement	Signature by the holder of a negotiable instrument, usually upon the reverse side thereof, for he purpose of conveying that instrument to another, in consideration of value received in exchange.
inducement	Anything said, done or offered for the purpose of causing another to act or to refrain from acting in a particular manner in reliance upon, or in consideration of, such statement, action or offering.
inducement letter	A short-form contract or deal memo in the form of a letter, committing the writer to perform certain obligations, usually in respect to a particular project or contract. Such letters are often used to demonstrate that the writer is "attached" to a prospective project, for the purpose of soliciting the participation of others, or to aid in obtaining financial backing. (See also, "commitment letter" and "side letter.")
infancy	In law, the condition of being below the age of legal maturity.
inference	Process of reasoning by which a fact or proposition is deduced as being a logical consequence flowing from other facts or conditions already proven or admitted.

information and belief	Phrase often used in legal pleadings (*i.e.,* in complaints, answers, and declarations) by which a person states a fact not upon the basis of personal knowledge, but upon the basis that the person has information and a belief that the fact stated is true. Conversely, a lack of information or belief as to the truth of a particular allegation can be used as grounds to deny the truth thereof, upon that basis.
informed consent	Agreement to do something or to allow something to happen, after having been fully apprised of the possible consequences thereof.
infra	Literally "below." *(Latin)* Used to indicate that certain referenced material is to be located at a later point in the same document. (See also, *"ante"* and *"supra"*)
infraction	Violation of a rule, regulation or ordinance, or violation of a statute which provides that such violation is less than a misdemeanor. (*E.g.,* Some Vehicle Code violations may be infractions, rather than misdemeanors.)
infringe	To trespass or encroach upon the rights or property of another, particularly with respect to intellectual property.
infringement	In copyright and patent law, the unlawful use of another's protected intellectual property. Generally, any unlawful use or entry upon the rights or property of another.
ingress	Entrance. The right to enter or the act of entering.
inherent	Implicit. Automatically included. Descriptive of a quality or condition which is always present within something else. Integrated into and a constant part of a larger whole.
inherit	To receive all or a portion of the estate of a deceased person.

inheritance	That which one lawfully receives upon the death of another.
initial public offering	The first general issue of corporate stock or securities for sale to the public. Usually referred to by the acronym, "IPO."
injunction	A court order compelling someone to do something or to refrain from doing something.
injunctive relief	Type of judicial remedy in which one seeks not damages but rather a court order compelling or prohibiting certain actions by another.
injunctive relief provision	Contract language by which the parties may stipulate as to whether injunctive relief will or will not be an available remedy against a particular party with respect to contract performance. The contract may also seek to waive or to limit the amount of any court-imposed bond as a condition of an injunction. Such limitations and waivers are judicially disfavored, and may be avoided by the court, depending on the jurisdiction and the facts of a particular case.
injury	Harm done to a person by the acts or omissions of another.
innocent	Without guilt. A verdict of "not guilty" is not equivalent to a factual finding of innocence, since the verdict reflects only that the prosecution has failed to prove guilt beyond a reasonable doubt. In certain rare circumstances, a court may enter a factual finding of innocence, fully restoring the reputation of an acquitted defendant.
inquest	Investigation and/or a hearing conducted by the coroner to determine cause of death.

INS	Acronym for Immigration and Naturalization Service, an agency of the U.S. government which has been merged into the Department of Homeland Security as part of the U.S. Citizenship and Immigration Services (USCIS). See "DHS."
insanity	In law, mental illness of such a severe nature that a person cannot distinguish right from wrong, and is therefore a danger to him- or herself and to society at large, and cannot be allowed to remain at liberty. A condition which negates the affected person's legal responsibility and capacity. See *mens rea*.
insert	A printed, removable portion of record packaging, usually in booklet form. In CD jewel case packaging, the cover of the insert is also the front cover of the album, visible through the plastic face of the case. (See "inset card" and "jewel case." See also, "J-card.")
inset card	A printed, non-removable portion of record packaging. In CD jewel case packaging, the cover of the inset card is the rear cover of the album, sandwiched between a usually-opaque CD holder and the transparent back face of the case. Bar codes, credits and copyright notices generally appear on the inset card. The folded edge of the inset card is also the edge label of the jewel case. (See "insert" and "jewel case.")
insider	One who has a position in a business, stock brokerage, financial institution, or other organization which provides that person with access to information relating to stock values in advance of the time when such information would become available to the public at large. Insiders are forbidden by law from using such information for their own or others' benefit, and are subject to criminal penalties for so doing.
insider trading	Crime of using confidential information obtained by an insider about a business for the purpose of buying or selling stock at a profit.
insolvency	Condition of having more liability than assets.

inspection of documents	In discovery, the right to examine and copy the opposing party's documentary and tangible property.
installment contract	Type of agreement calling for periodic performance and payments.
instigate	To bring about, initiate or incite others to take some particular action.
instrument	Any written legal document such as a contract, lease, deed, bond, certificate, or will.
insufficient evidence	Finding by a court that the evidence produced and admitted is inadequate to justify a verdict in favor of the party offering that evidence. Grounds for dismissal, non-suit, directed verdict or NOV.
insurance	Contract whereby one party, for consideration, agrees to compensate the other party for loss incurred as a result of specified perils up to specified limits.
insured	Person or entity whose loss will be compensated under a policy of insurance, although not necessarily the person or entity which will receive payment therefor. See "beneficiary" "co-insured" and "loss payee")
insurer	An insurance company.
intangible property	Items which represent value but which have no intrinsic worth themselves, such as stock in a company.
integration	Adopting a writing as part of another by express language, such that both writings are a necessary part of the entire agreement. The two (or more) writings are then said to be "wholly integrated." Integration is to be distinguished from "incorporation by reference" where the referenced document is not interdependent with the new document.
intent	Mental desire and will to act in a particular way.

inter alia	Literally, "among other things" *(Latin)*
inter vivos	Literally, "between (among) the living" *(Latin)* Any transaction in which all parties are alive is an *inter vivos* transaction.
inter vivos trust	Trust created to receive and thereafter own assets of a living person (trustor or settlor), for the benefit of that person and/or his or her family (as beneficiary) and usually under his or her control (as trustee) for the duration of his or her life, whereupon the deceased is succeeded by a new, designated trustee and, if there were no previous co-beneficiaries, by new designated beneficiaries. A legal device which avoids probate and substantial tax liabilities upon the death of the trustor. Colloquially referred to as a "living trust."
interest	(1) A total or partial right to property. (2) Money charged or earned, based upon a percentage of a sum borrowed, lent, or deposited.
interim	Interval between two events.
interim order	A temporary court order, in effect only until a full hearing or trial can be held upon the subject issue, or until a particular date.
interlineation	Act of writing between the lines of a document, usually to insert minor modifications or addenda, and generally initialed by the parties executing the document to indicate their agreement to the change.
interlocutory	Provisional and not intended to be final.
interpleader	Procedure by which a person holding property, but not asserting an interest in that property, may surrender it to the court in a case involving that property, so that proper distribution thereof may be adjudicated as between the litigants who do assert an interest therein.

interregnum	Literally, the period between the death (or abdication or overthrow) of a reigning monarch, and the crowning of his or her successor. More commonly, any period between one leader losing power and another leader assuming power, whether in government, business, or other organization. A period between governments.
interrogation	Questioning of a suspect or witness by law enforcement authorities.
interrogatories	Written questions propounded by one party to another as part of the discovery process in litigation.
interstate commerce	Commercial traffic, trade, business, movement of persons, goods, property or money between two or more states.
intervene	Voluntarily obtaining permission of the court to become a party in a lawsuit in which one was not named as a party, but in the outcome of which one has substantial interest.
intervening cause	An event which occurs between the original improper or dangerous act, and the apparent ultimate result of that act, such that the original actor may be relieved of liability on the ground that it was the intervening (rather than the original) cause which proximately resulted in the loss, damage or harm suffered.
intervention	Procedure by which a third party may, by court order, join as a party in ongoing litigation.
intestacy	Condition of having died without a valid will.
intestate	One who is without a will.
intestate succession	The rules governing inheritance of the estate of a person who died without a will.

intrinsic fraud	Intentionally false representation, as by perjury, false instruments, or by concealment or misrepresentation of evidence, which occurs within the framework of actual conduct of trial and pertains to and affects the determination of issues presented therein.
instant	This specific document, matter, pleading or proceeding which is currently under consideration. *E.g.,* the instant contract, or the instant motion.
internecine	Relating to conflict within a family or group. An internal dispute.
inure	To take effect; to result in. To become to the benefit of.
invasion of privacy	Intrusion into the personal life of another.
invest	To put money into a business or to buy property or securities.
investment	Money put into use for profit, or the property or business interest acquired thereby.
invitee	One who comes onto another's property, premises or place of business by express or implied invitation.
involuntary	Without intent, will or choice.
IPO	See "initial public offering."
ips	Inches per second. Used to designate the capstan speed at which tape passes the recording or playback head.
ipse dixit	Literally, "he himself said it" *(Latin)*, refers to a bare assertion, based solely upon the statement of an individual.

ipso facto	Literally, "by the fact" *(Latin)*, refers to a fact that is self-demonstrating.
irreducible	Not capable of being resolved or further simplified.
irrelevant	Not important, pertinent, material or germane to the matter at hand.
irreparable damage	Harm which cannot be undone and which no monetary compensation can cure.
irrevocable	Not capable of being revoked. A permanent commitment, which cannot later be retracted or cancelled.
issue	(1) Matter which is in dispute or under consideration. (2) An individual's children or other direct descendants.

J

J-card　Type of printed insert used in cassette and DAT jewel case packaging, it is in the approximate form of the letter "J" when viewed edgewise. It is generally printed on both sides, and may contain multiple folds at its longest side, which can be unfolded when the J-card is removed from the case. The short, edge, and face sides of the J-card are (respectively) the back, edge, and front covers of the recording. (See "jewel case.")

jeopardy　Peril, particularly a danger of being convicted of a crime.

jewel case　Clear plastic case used to package CDs, cassettes, and other media.

jingle　Original or derivative musical composition used for broadcast advertising. Music used in a commercial or spot.

JNOV　Judgment in favor of one party, notwithstanding a contrary jury verdict in favor of the other party. In criminal matters, a judgment of acquittal, overriding a jury verdict for conviction. (See "NOV")

jobber　A merchant who buys products (usually in bulk or in lots) and markets them to retailers.

John Doe　Fictitious name used for a possible male defendant whose true name is unknown at the time of pleading.

join　Adoption by a person or party of a position advanced by another person or party, supporting that position without the necessity of restating essentially identical material.

joinder　Uniting two or more things into one. Consolidation.

joinder of issue	That point in a lawsuit when the defendant has admitted and/or denied plaintiff's various allegations of fact, whereupon the issues are said to have been joined, and the denied facts to be "at-issue."
joint	Referring to property, rights or obligations which are held by two or more persons, with each holding an undivided interest in the whole thereof.
joint and several	Referring to an obligation or a judgment for which two or more people are each individually liable for the entire obligation, not merely a proportional share.
jointly and severally	Phrase used to indicate that two or more persons are being categorized as a single entity, so that reference to such entity refers to them each singly (*i.e.*, "severally") while at the same time treating them as a common (*i.e.*, "joint") entity. Phrase may be used in contracts where multiple individuals appear as a single party, as well as individually. *E.g.*, "John Doe, Robert Roe, and George Spelvin (hereinafter jointly and severally 'Artist')." Phrase may also appear in court judgments, where multiple parties are made "jointly and severally" liable for payment of the judgment amount.
joint custody	Condition in which two or more persons have co-equal rights to possession and control of a thing. In marital dissolution actions, when both parents retain equal legal custody with respect to minor children of the marriage, with physical custody primarily with one parent or the other.
joint liability	When two or more persons are responsible for an obligation or duty. When a monetary obligation is performed by only one of them, he or she may seek to recover from the others their proportional share under the doctrine of contribution.
joint tenancy	Manner of holding title to property wherein each joint tenant owns an undivided interest in the whole, rather than a distinct percentage. This is a crucial distinction, as compared to "tenancy in common," particularly with respect to tax and inheritance issues.

joint venture	Enterprise entered into by two or more persons or entities for profit.
judgment (judgement)	The final decision by a court in a lawsuit, criminal prosecution, or upon submission to the court of an arbitrator's award.
judgment by default	Judgment entered at plaintiff's request against a named defendant who, having been duly served, has failed to timely respond to plaintiff's allegations.
judgment creditor	The prevailing party in a lawsuit to whom the court has awarded monetary compensation.
judgment debt	Amount of money in a judgment award to the prevailing party.
judgment debtor	The defeated party in a lawsuit against whom the court has awarded monetary damages.
judicial	Referring to a judge, court or the court system.
judicial discretion	Power of the judge to make decisions on some matters based solely on his own perceptions.
judicial economy	Doctrine which urges attorneys and the court to eliminate or minimize duplication of effort, in order to avoid unnecessarily imposing on the court's time.
judicial foreclosure	Judgment by a court ordering the sheriff to conduct a foreclosure sale of real property for the purpose of paying an obligation.
judicial notice	Process by which the Court accepts as fact certain matters which are presented to the court for that purpose. Matters subject to judicial notice include (but are not limited to) published laws, court records, official government documents, and facts of general knowledge which are universally accepted as being true. (*E.g.,* the court will take judicial notice that the sun sets in the west.)

judicial policy	A general doctrine reflecting courts' preferences in respect to discretionary matters. *E.g.,* Judicial policy favors having matters determined upon their merits rather than by default, and therefor urges that defaults be set aside, whenever legally permissible.
judicial proceedings	Any official action by or before a judge, commissioner, or magistrate.
judicial sale	Sale of goods by a court official or designee (keeper, trustee or sheriff), pursuant to a court order. Judicial sales may be post-judgment (to satisfy judgment debt) or pre-judgment (to liquidate perishable, attached (seized) property, to avoid waste.)
jurat	That portion of an affidavit in which a notary public attests that an oath has been duly administered to the affiant, who has sworn thereunder as to the truth of the matters averred in the affidavit.
Juris Doctor (J.D.)	Law degree awarded upon graduation by many schools of law.
jurisdiction	Authority given by law to a court to try and adjudicate cases, and to enforce its rulings.
jurisprudence	The overall science and philosophy of law.
jurist	Generally, any attorney or legal scholar, but popularly used to refer to a judge.
juror	Person who actually serves on a jury. *Cf.* "venire"
jury	Panel of citizens who hear, deliberate upon, and decide the facts of a case at trial.
jury box	Demised area in which the jury sits in assigned seats during judicial proceedings
jury fees	Rather minimal amount paid each day to jurors.

jury panel	List from which jurors for a particular trial may be selected. See "venire."
jury selection	Process by which a jury is chosen, with a panel of potential jurors being interviewed by the court and/or by the parties' attorneys. See *"voir dire."*
jury tampering	Crime of attempting to influence a jury through any means outside the scope of regular proceedings at trial.
jury trial	Trial of a lawsuit or criminal prosecution in which the issues of fact are tried by a jury.
justice of the peace	A judge who, in some jurisdictions, handles minor legal matters such as misdemeanors, small claims, and civil marriage ceremonies.
justiciable	Capable of being decided by legal proceedings.

K

K.	Attorneys' shorthand symbol for "contract."
kangaroo court	Sham proceeding, organized as a court but without legal basis or authority.
key man clause	Contract provision which allows artist to terminate contract with label in the event that certain expressly-named employees of the label (*e.g.*, a particular producer, A&R representative, or other person the artist believes is essential to his or her success) become unavailable to work with the artist, ether by termination of their employment, or otherwise. Generally, the provision is intended to allow the artist the option to follow such designated person to his or her new employer's label.
key man insurance	Specialized insurance policy purchased by a business to protect it on the death or disability of a valued employee. In partnerships, such insurance is frequently acquired to provide funds with which surviving partner(s) may purchase the deceased's partnership interest from his or her estate. (See, "buy-sell agreement.")
keystoning	Practice of setting sale price by doubling purchase price. A 100% markup (50% profit margin.)
kickback	Payment back of a portion of the purchase price to the buyer, an employee of the buyer, or a public official by the seller, to induce the purchase or to improperly influence future purchases. A bribe. Such payments are not tax deductible as ordinary and necessary business expenses. Such payments are frequently held to be criminal in nature.
kidnaping (kidnapping)	The taking of a person against his or her will, by force, threat of force, trick, incapacitation, or other means. The taking of a minor without consent of the legal guardian.
kin	Blood relatives.

kindred	Literally, blood relatives. Colloquially, a sense of relatedness or similarity between persons or things.
knew or should have known	Phrase alleging that a person either had actual knowledge of some matter, or (alternatively) contending that, under the circumstance presented and a duty owed, a reasonable person would have had actual knowledge of that matter, and that actual knowledge should therefore be presumed, as a matter of law. (See, "*scienter.*")
known and unknown	Phrase used to expand scope of document beyond what may be expressed. The phrase is most frequently seen in recording contracts to preserve the label's right to produce commercial recordings in media not available (or invented) at the time of the contract. (*i.e.,* "in all media, whether now known or unknown..") It is also found in general releases which ask the releasing party to give up all claims "whether known or unknown."

L

£   Currency symbol for British pounds. Since February 1971, the pound has been decimalized, with 100 pennies ("new pence") to the pound. The prior system, which may still appear in older documents, was based on 12 (old) pence to the shilling and 20 shillings to the pound. For conversion, 1 shilling equals 5 new pence, and one old pence equals 5/12 (or 0.4167) new pence.

label   A record company, or division of a record company, generally identifiable by a particular trademarked name (*e.g.,* "Capitol Records") appearing on the commercial recordings which it releases. (See "major.")

laches   Equitable doctrine stating that a legal right or claim will not be enforced when the person holding that right or claim has, for an appreciable period of time, knowingly permitted others to violate that right or claim, without taking action, to the point where that lack of action was reasonably perceived and relied upon by affected persons as being acquiescence, a waiver, or permission in respect to that right or claim.

land   Real property, and all that grows thereon.

landlocked   Real property which is surrounded on all sides by others' privately-owned property, with no direct or legal access to public streets or roads. Property which has no lawful means of ingress or egress (*i.e.,* no easement.) See "easement."

landlord   Person who owns real property and rents or leases it to others (tenants.)

landlord / tenant   That area of law concerning the renting and leasing of real property.

Lanham Act More formally known as the Trademark Act of 1946, the Lanham Act (15 U.S.C.§§ 1051, *et seq.*) contains federal statutes governing trademark law in the United States. The Act is not the sole source of U.S. trademark law, since both common law and state statutes also control some aspects of trademark protection.

lapse To pass slowly, silently, or by degrees. To deviate from, or fail to perform, a duty or obligation. To fall into disuse. To expire.

larceny Crime of taking property of another without permission. Theft. (See, "conversion.")

last clear chance A legal doctrine which imposes a duty to exercise ordinary care to avoid injury to another who has inadvertently and unknowingly placed him- or herself in peril. Not imposed equally in all jurisdictions, the doctrine is generally applied in accident cases with respect to contributory negligence issues.

last will and testament An ornate and redundant way of saying "will."

latent defect A hidden flaw, weakness or imperfection in a product, property or document which could not reasonably have been discovered through initial inspection, but only through specialized knowledge or testing beyond the scope of ordinary care and diligence. A concealed defect or design flaw which, although always present, only manifests itself after a passage of time or under extreme but not unforeseeable conditions. (*Cf.,* "patent defect")

lateral support The right of a landowner to assurance that adjacent property will not be excavated in such a manner as would adversely affect the stability of his or her property.

law Any system of regulations to govern the conduct of the populace within the jurisdiction of those regulations.

law and motion	Procedural and other matters heard by the court in regard to a case, prior to commencement of trial. In some jurisdictions, a special "law and motion" department is designated for hearing such matters.
law of the case	Once a judge has decided a legal question during the conduct of a case, that decision becomes "law" with respect to that case, unless reversed or modified by the judge or by a higher court.
lawsuit	Common term for a legal action by one or more persons or entities against one or more others.
lawyer	A person trained in the law. A legal scholar. Colloquially, an attorney-at-law, although while all attorneys are lawyers, not all lawyers are necessarily attorneys. (*Cf.*, "attorney-at-law.")
leading question	Objectionable form of question which contains within it the preferred answer. (*E.g.,* "Isn't it true that you've known defendant for more than 20 years?") Leading questions are permitted on cross-examination or when questioning hostile witnesses.
leadsheet	Written page(s) setting forth the lyrics, melody and chords of a musical composition.
lease	Written agreement in which the owner of property grants the use of that property to another for consideration and for a fixed period of time.
leasehold	Real estate which is the subject of a lease.
leaving man clause (leaving member clause)	Contract provision which sets forth rights and obligations between members of a musical performance group in the event that one or more members leaves the group, particularly with respect to future royalty participation of leaving member(s). Leaving member provisions also appear in recording contracts, enumerating rights and obligations of the record label and of the group in the event of a member's departure.

legal	According to law; not in violation of law or public policy.
legal action	Any lawsuit, petition or prosecution.
legal age	The age at which a person is deemed responsible for his or her own conduct.
legal duty	Responsibility owed to others to act in accordance with law.
legal fiction	An assumption of fact adopted by the court for convenience in deciding a legal question. (*E.g.* that a corporation is a "person.")
legal tender	Money.
legalese	Colloquial term for arcane, convoluted, obfuscatory, and specialized language used by lawyers.
legate	A limited-purpose representative; a messenger.
legislative intent	The purpose of the legislature in enacting any particular law; the intended function and effect of a law. In interpreting a statute, the court may look to the legislative intent underlying that law to assist in determining how that law should be applied.
legitimate	Legal, proper, genuine; real.
less returns	Phrase used in contracts to provide that royalties will be paid based on the number of units ultimately sold, rather than all units "manufactured and distributed."
lessee	Person renting property under a lease.
lesser-included offense	In criminal law, a crime which is proven by the same facts which prove the greater, charged offense.
lessor	Owner of property who rents it to a another (the lessee) pursuant to a lease.

let	To allow or permit.
letter of credit	Document issued by a bank guaranteeing to provide a customer with funds up to a certain amount.
letter of direction	Instruction specifying the manner in which all or part of an obligation is to be paid, and to whom. Generally, a letter of direction is used to provide direct payments to a manager or other person contractually entitled to receive a portion of an artist's royalty payments.
leverage	Purchase in which all or part of the purchase price is obtained by giving security against assets of the property being acquired thereby. The most common and familiar form of leveraged purchase is real estate, where all or a portion of the purchase monies are from loans secured by deeds of trust recorded against the property being purchased.
levy	To seize (take) property pursuant to a court order or other legal process.
liability	A broad legal term, liability generally refers to an assignment to particular person(s) of legal responsibility for conduct, actions, conditions, circumstances and other matters for which the law deems them accountable to the public at large, or to specific persons.
liable	Responsible; obligated; accountable.
libel	Publication of false, defamatory material about another by means of print or images.
libel *per se*	Broadcast or written publication of a false, defamatory statement about another person.
liberty	Freedom from restraint and the power to follow one's own will.

Library of Congress	Governmental agency which is responsible for accepting registration of copyrights, maintaining copyright records, accepting deposits of royalty payments, and generally administrating all matters related to copyrights.
license	Permission to perform a particular act.
licensee	Person who is given a license.
licensor	Person who gives another a license.
lien	Claim or charge against property or funds for goods or services rendered in regard to that property. Anyone wh performs work on a project may be entitled to enforce a lien against that project.
lienor	Person who holds a lien on another's property or funds.
lieu	Stead. Place. Substitute. Almost invariably preceded by the word "in." Thus "in lieu of" means "instead of" or "in the place of."
life estate	Right to use or occupy property for one's lifetime.
limitation of actions	Period of time during which a person must commence a lawsuit upon certain causes of action. The period of time varies by jurisdiction and by the nature of the action.
limited jurisdiction	Courts' authority over only certain types of cases (*e.g.,* bankruptcy) or over cases asserting no more than a certain amount of damages (*e.g.,* small claims courts)
limited liability company	Form of business organization comprised of one or more members (investors), operated by one or more managers (officers), having liability-shielding and other characteristics similar to a corporation, but with the advantage that its profits are taxed only as personal income of its members. Generally abbreviated "LLC"

limited liability partnership	A specialized form of partnership available only to certain specified professions (*e.g.,* law, accountancy, architecture) requiring maintenance of certain levels of insurance, *inter alia.*
limited partnership	A special type of partnership, usually comprised of one or more "general" partners, and one or more "limited" partners (investors), who do not participate in the operations or management of the business and who are shielded from any personal liability for the business' obligations beyond the potential loss of their investment.
liquidate	To sell the assets of a business, converting all of its assets to "liquid" form (*i.e.,* to cash).
liquidated damages	A sum of money agreed upon by both parties to a contract as being the exact sum (and no more) which will be satisfactory compensation in the event of a failure of performance.
liner notes	Written text provided along with an album, generally as part of an insert or other packaging element, which contain narrative, historical and biographical information concerning the album, group or artist. Liner notes may be separately copyrighted as text.
lis pendens	Literally, "a lawsuit pending" *(Latin),* a written notice which is recorded against real property title, giving constructive notice to all persons that a suit has been commenced which, if successful, will directly affect title to that real property. The effect of a *lis pendens* is to chill the marketability of the property, since any potential buyers or lenders are on notice that the owner may not be able to deliver good title, and their purchase monies or loan collateral may be lost to them if the plaintiff's suit is successful.
literary property	The writings of an author.

litigant	Any named party in a lawsuit. Includes the owners of partnerships and proprietorships, but does <u>not</u> include the attorneys, witnesses, court officers, or the officers, directors or employees of corporate parties.
litigation	A lawsuit or other resort to the courts to determine a question of fact or of law.
litigious	Referring to one who constantly brings or prolongs litigation.
living trust	See "*inter vivos* trust"
living will	Also called "a durable power of attorney," a document stating a person's wishes regarding medical care in the event that he or she becomes incapacitated, and designating someone to make medical decisions on his or her behalf in such eventuality.
loan out	Arrangement in which an entity, such as a corporation, enters into a contract wherein it agrees to provide the other party with the services of an artist or other person. Usually, the contracting entity is owned or controlled by the person whose services are being lent out, who is not personally a party to the loan-out agreement. Loan-out agreements are generally used for tax- and estate-planning purposes. (See "side letter.")
LOC	Library of Congress
lockout	(1) Labor dispute tactic in which employer ceases operation during dispute, "locking out" employees and thereby stopping their employment income.
	(2) Arrangement with rehearsal or recording studio providing for 24-hour-per-day exclusive use of facility so that equipment can remain in place between sessions.

lodged	Presented, deposited or left for safekeeping. Pleadings or other documents deposited with the court but which are not deemed to have been "filed," and which are therefore not entered on the docket, are referred to as having been "lodged."
logo	A unique iconic emblem and/or type-style, adopted by a business, group, or individual as an identifying mark. (See also, "trademark.")
long-arm statutes	Laws which permit a state court to exercise jurisdiction over persons or entities not residents of that state but who or which have conducted transactions or engaged in conduct within that state which are a subject of the relevant case.
long cause matter	Lawsuit in which it is estimated that trial will take a prolonged period of time.
loop	To record new dialogue to replace the original (production) recording for a video or film. See "dub" and "ADR (2)."
loss	Broad term, roughly equivalent to "damage" and "harm," it is the compensable value placed on injury or damages suffered due to the conduct of another.
loss payee	Person designated to receive payment of claim benefits under an insurance policy.
lower court	Any court of relatively lesser rank within a judicial system.
lyricist	Author of the word (lyrics) intended to be integrated with music, thereby creating a song. When a song is written contemporaneously by a musical composer and lyricist, they each share equally in the indivisible whole, with each considered a coauthor of the other's contribution, unless there is a specific agreement between them to the contrary. (*Cf.,* "composer." See also, "songwriter.")

M

M. O.

Acronym for *modus operandi (Latin)*. Literally, one's method (mode) of operating. An habitual or repeated manner or pattern of behavior. The way in which one generally or invariably performs a particular task.

magistrate

Generically, any judge of a court. In the federal court system, a judge who presides over certain procedural matters, and who is of a lower rank than a district court judge.

Magna Carta

Literally "Great Charter" *(Latin)* the Magna Carta (or Magna Charta) was signed by King John in 1215, and is generally regarded as the foundation of all subsequent English and American constitutional rights. Note however the distinction between a charter (rights granted by a higher, sovereign authority) and a constitution (rights declared by the people, for themselves.)

mailed

A letter, package, notice, or other material is deemed to have been "mailed" when it is properly packaged, addressed, bears prepaid postage in full, and has been deposited into an authorized mail receptacle.

maim

To inflict a serious bodily injury, including crippling or mutilation.

major

Short for "major label." One of the established record companies having its own distribution system, as distinct from an "independent label" or "distributed label."

majority (1)

Age at which a person can thereafter exercise all normal legal rights.

majority (2)

A number greater than half of the total number. (*Cf.,* "plurality")

make	(1) To create something. (2) To sign a check, promissory note, or other negotiable instrument.
make whole	To pay or award damages sufficient to put the party who was injured in the same or equivalent position to that which they would have enjoyed but for the injury.
maker	Person who signs a check or promissory note.
malfeasance	Intentionally doing something which is either legally or morally wrong.
malice	The intentional doing of a wrongful act, without just cause or excuse, either with actual intent to cause injury, or under circumstance where the law will presume evil intent.
malice aforethought	Conscious intent to cause harm, prior to or while committing an act which causes harm.
malicious prosecution	Filing a lawsuit without probable cause, or with the actual intention of harassing or creating problems for adverse parties.
malpractice	An act or continuing conduct of a professional which does not comport with the rules of conduct for that profession. Professional negligence.
malum in se	Literally "wrong in itself" *(Latin)*, refers to an act which is universally deemed to be wrongful; that which is contrary to moral or natural law.(*E.g.*, theft; murder.)
malum prohibitum	Literally "wrong by prohibition" *(Latin)*, refers to an act which is wrong because the law says so. (*E.g.*, jaywalking, gambling; prostitution.)
manager	Person with control of a business, or of some part or aspect of a business, of such apparent authority that a reasonable inference may be drawn that such person is authorized to exercise personal discretion in making management decisions for that business. (See also "business manager" and "personal manager.")

mandamus	Literally, "we command" *(Latin)*, a writ originating from a court to a public officer, public entity, or court of lower jurisdiction, ordering performance of some act specified in the writ. Also and more frequently referred to as a "writ of mandate."
mandate	Any mandatory order or requirement under statute, regulation, ordinance, or court order. A requirement.
mandatory	That which is absolutely demanded or required.
mandatory settlement conference	In litigation, a court ordered attempt to resolve disputes prior to trial, generally presided over by a judge other than the judge who will try the case. Abbreviated with the acronym, "MSC."
manifest	(1) Completely obvious or self-evident to the senses, particularly to sight. Clear, visible, unmistakable, indisputable. (2) A written document listing the contents of a shipment.
Mann Act	Federal statute making it a crime to transport a woman across state lines for "immoral purposes."
manslaughter	Unlawful killing of another person without premeditation.
maritime law	That body of law which deals with occurrences at sea. Also referred to as "admiralty law" or "the law of the sea," maritime law can become a factor in performance contracts relating to cruise ships. (See "choice of law.")
margin	An amount above (or below) a specified point or amount, generally expressed as a percentage of the total amount. (*Cf.*, "markup.")
marginal	Of only minor importance or relevance.

mark	Usually an "X" made by a person who is illiterate or too weak to sign his or her name, generally countersigned by a witness who can attest as to the identity of the maker of the mark, and as to such mark having been that person's voluntary act at a certain time and place.
marked for identification	Documents or objects produced during a trial, but not yet admitted into evidence.
market value	Price which a seller of property would receive in an open market sale of that property. (See "FMV.")
marketable title	Title to property which has no encumbrances.
markup	The amount added to costs to arrive at a selling price. It may be expressed as a percentage of the underlying costs, so that a 100% markup results in a 50% profit margin. (*Cf.,* "margin.")
master	(1) An employer. (2) See "master recording."
master and servant	Body of law which governs employer-employee relations.
master recording	A storage medium (analogue tape, DAT, CD or other medium) containing the final, mixed, balanced and equalized tracks of a recorded album or composition, from which commercial copies may thereafter be reproduced. It is a copy of the master recording, or a compilation of several such master recordings, which is submitted to the Copyright Office (along with Form SR) as a "phonorecord" for a registered Sound Recording ("℗") copyright.
master use license	Agreement permitting the use of a preexisting master recording. Such license conveys rights to use only the recording itself, and does not convey rights with respect to the musical composition or other copyrighted material embodied in the recording. (See "sync license" and "synchronization rights.")

material	(1) Relevant and significant. (2) Having physical existence.
material representation	Convincing, relevant statement made to induce someone to enter into an agreement or transaction.
material witness	Person who apparently has information about the subject matter of a case which no one else, or very few, could provide as testimony. In certain criminal cases, material witnesses may be held in custody, against their will, under a special warrant issued for that purpose.
matrix	A material environment in which something is maintained, developed or shaped. A mechanical medium from which a phonorecord can be manufactured.
matter of record	Anything uttered in open court and transcribed, or filed with the court, including testimony, evidence, rulings, argument, objections and pleadings.
maturity	The date upon which payment of a principal amount owed becomes due.
maxims	A collection of legal truisms.
may	A permissive instruction. A choice to act or to not act, as distinct from the mandatory "must" or "shall." The distinction between the permissive "may" and the mandatory "shall" is critical in interpreting contracts, orders, and statutes.
mayhem	Criminal act of disabling, disfiguring or cutting another.
MCPS	Acronym for "Mechanical-Copyright Protection Society," a not-for-profit performing rights organization which grants licenses and collects royalties for composers, songwriters and music publishers in the U.K.

MCPS-PRS Alliance	Management entity owned by MCPS and PRS, jointly, and which manages the common activities and services of both non-profit societies. (See "MCPS" and "PRS")
mdse.	Abbreviation of "merchandise."
mechanic's lien	Right of a craftsman, laborer, supplier, architect, engineer or contractor to encumber title to real property, pending satisfactions in full of sums owed for services rendered in respect to the subject property. For materials delivered to the property, the lien is more properly referred to as a "Materialman's Lien."
mechanical license	License granted by owner of copyright to composition, permitting licensee to commercially record and release that composition for royalty rate and/or fee, and within a particular territory, as specified within the license. (See "compulsory license" and "incept license.")
media	Plural of "medium." (1) Colloquially, all journalistic outlets, including all print (newspapers & magazines) and broadcast (TV and radio) organizations. (2) Agencies, devices, or substances by means of which something is recorded, conveyed, transmitted, reproduced or transferred. Thus CDs, vinyl discs and cassette tapes are each a distinct medium for transmitting commercial sound recordings, and collectively they are media for such recordings. (See "known and unknown.")
mediation	Method for attempting informal resolution of a legal dispute through the active participation of a third party (the mediator) who acts as an impartial conduit between opposing parties, seeking to develop mutually-acceptable terms of compromise.
mediator	Person who conducts mediation.

meet and confer	Requirement of courts that before certain types of motions are filed, the parties or their counsel must seek an informal resolution of the salient issue between themselves.
meeting of the minds	A common understanding between contracting parties as to the terms of their contract.
memorandum	A brief writing, note, summary or outline.
mens rea	Literally "guilty mind" *(Latin)* The ability to formulate a criminal intent is an essential element of criminal conduct. One who unable to form such intent cannot be lawfully convicted of a crime.
mental anguish	Mental suffering which includes fright, feelings of distress, humiliation, embarrassment, and anxiety.
mercantile law	Also called commercial law, that broad area of the law dealing with business, commerce and trade.
merchandise	(1) Goods or products offered for sale or as promotional materials. (2) To offer such goods or products for sale or as part of a promotional campaign.
merchandising	The right to manufacture and market products bearing the image, logo, or other elements related to an artist, group, project, company or organization for commercial gain, as an exploitation of commercial success of the underlying property, or to promote or enhance such commercial success. (See also, "tie-in.")
merchantable	That which is in a condition suitable for sale.
merger	The joining together of two or more business entities into one, generally referred to thereafter as the "surviving" entity. An entity which has ceased independent existence through merger into another is said to have been "merged out."

mesne	Literally "middle" (Norman French), refers to an intermediate or intervening condition or transaction. The middle between two extremes, particularly with respect to time or rank.
mesne conveyance	An intermediate conveyance, wherein title or delivery is taken for the purpose of re-conveying the same to another.
mesne profits	Profits which have accrued while there was a dispute over their eventual distribution.
metes and bounds	Surveyor's description of a parcel of real property, giving location, orientation, and lengths of the boundaries of such property. A legal description of real property.
MIDEM	Annual, five-day international music marketplace for all genres of music which is held in Cannes, France, usually in late January.
ministerial act	An act performed by a governmental employee, in furtherance of a legal requirement or court order, without any intervention of that employee's own judgment or initiative.
minor	One who is under legal age.
minority	(1) A number which is less than one half of a total number. (2) A group defined by common ethnicity, religion, gender, age, sexual orientation or other criteria, which constitutes only a fractional percentage of the general populace within a particular area.
minutes	Written record of meetings, particularly of boards of directors of corporations.
misadventure	That which results from an unintentional accident without any violation of law.

misappropriation	Intentional, illegal use of the property or funds of another.
misdemeanor	A crime deemed of less severity than a felony, punishable by a fine and/or county jail time not exceeding one year.
misfeasance	Management of a business, public office or other responsibility in a less-than-ideal or improper manner. (See also, "malfeasance" and "nonfeasance")
misjoinder	Inclusion in a lawsuit of parties (as plaintiffs or defendants) or of causes of action which are found to not be properly a part of that suit.
misnomer	A inappropriate name, at odds with the nature of the thing.
misprision of a felony	Crime of concealing another's felony, but without such previous connection or subsequent assistance as would elevate the crime to that of accessory before or after the fact.
misrepresentation	The crime or tort of misstating facts to obtain money, goods or benefits from another through their detrimental reliance upon the supposed truth of those alleged facts. Misrepresentation of material facts, whether intentional or negligent, may constitute actionable fraud.
mistake	Error in comprehending facts, meaning of words, or the consequences of some act or failure to act.
mistrial	Termination of a trial before its normal conclusion due to some extraordinary event which cannot be rectified in the course of continuing that trial.
mitigating circumstances	In criminal law, conditions or happenings which do not excuse the crime, but which may be taken into account as reducing the degree of moral culpability of the accused., and at the time of sentencing.

mitigation of damages	Legal requirement that someone injured by another has a duty to exercise reasonable diligence and ordinary care in seeking to minimize the damage suffered.
modification	Change made to that which had previously existed, usually to accommodate changed or newly-discovered circumstances.
modus operandi	See M.O.
molestation	Crime of sexual acts with child under a certain age, as specified by statute.
monopoly	Business or inter-related group of businesses which controls all or nearly all of a particular field, business, industry, or resource.
month-to-month	Referring to a tenancy in which the tenant pays monthly, and without a lease. A written contract for month-to-month tenancies is generally referred to as a "Rental Agreement." (See also, "holdover tenancy.")
monument	(1) An established landmark which a surveyor uses as a point of reference in conducting a land survey. (2) An object or structure erected to commemorate some person, event or ideal.
moot	That which cannot be resolved by debate. Pointless. Unresolvable. A matter raised for argument's sake alone, not for resolution. An unsettled issue. Conversely, alternative solutions offered in respect to an issue which has already been thoroughly resolved.
moot court	Exercise regularly conducted in law schools in which a moot or hypothetical case is presented and argued.
moot point	A legal question which no court has decided, and which therefore remains unresolved. Colloquially, a point which isn't worth raising or arguing about.

moral certainty	That degree of certainty which would lead a reasonable person to act without hesitation or doubt. In criminal trials, the degree of certainty which jurors are required to achieve in order to vote for conviction.
moral turpitude	A gross violation of established standards of moral conduct; vileness; baseness; depravity. Willful disregard of moral or legal obligations to others.
morals clause	Contract provision which permits cancellation or suspension of the agreement, or which invokes penalties, in the event of conduct by a contracting party which is deemed to be contrary to good morals.
moratorium	A suspension of activity. A period of permissive or mandatory delay, generally to permit some act or obligation to be concluded, or for humanitarian purposes.
more prejudicial than probative	Rationale for exclusion of evidence, on ground that its emotional or sensational impact outweighs its relevance. *E.g.,* graphic photographs of a traffic fatality may be excluded because they are likely to incense or shock a jury, while having only little value as material evidence of elements necessary to the burden of proof.
moribund	Dying. In a state approaching death.
mortgage	Document in which the owner pledges title to real property as collateral for a loan, or as security for performance of some duty or obligation.
mortgagee	Person or business making a loan that is secured by a mortgage.
mortgagor	Person who has given a mortgage, pledging title to real property as security for a loan or other obligation.

most favored nation	Diplomatic phrase which has been carried over into business relationships, referring to an arrangement by which it is agreed that a party will not deal with the other party on terms which are less favorable than the terms afforded to any third party.
motion	Formal request made to a judge for an order or judgment.
motion for new trial	Post-trial request made by a defeated party for the case to be tried once again, from the beginning, on the grounds of some alleged legal defect in the proceedings.
motion for nonsuit	Trial motion by defendant for dismissal of case, after plaintiff has presented its case and rested, asserting that plaintiff failed to present evidence of all facts necessary to satisfy essential elements of plaintiff's causes of action.
motion for summary adjudication (of issues)	Also referred to (in some jurisdictions) as a "Motion for Partial Summary Judgment," a highly technical motion, subject to special procedural rules, wherein a party seeks to demonstrate that, based on matters of law and on facts which are not in dispute, the moving party is entitled to judgment, without trial, upon some (but not all) issues or causes of action which are at-issue in the case.
motion for summary judgment	Highly technical motion, subject to special procedural rules, wherein a party seeks to demonstrate that, based on matters of law and on facts which are not in dispute, the moving party is entitled to judgment, without trial, as to the entire case. Usually abbreviated by the acronym, "MSJ."
motion *in limine*	A motion made shortly before commencement of trial, generally for the purpose of excluding or limiting trial evidence and issues, by court order.
motion to strike	Motion for an order to eliminate all or a portion of a pleading or of testimony.

motion to suppress	Motion, generally on behalf of a criminal defendant, to exclude certain evidence or information from being introduced at trial, usually upon the ground that such evidence or information was obtained wrongfully, or derived from information unlawfully obtained. (See "fruit of the poisonous tree.")
motive	Probable reason why a person committed a particular act.
movant	The party making a motion.
move	To make a motion.
MPTF (1)	Motion Picture and Television Fund. A long-established charitable organization which provides financial assistance and care for actors and other members of the television and motion picture industry.
MPTF (2)	Music Performance Trust Funds. Trust funds established under the AFM contract which requires record companies to make contributions based on royalties due for record sales. The trust funds are disbursed by the various AFM locals to subsidize live performances.
MS	Standard abbreviation for "manuscript."
MSC	See "Mandatory Settlement Conference."
MSJ	See "Motion for Summary Judgment."
multinational	A business enterprise which has centers of operations in various countries, as distinguished from an "international" enterprise, which has its center of operations in one country, although it does business throughout the world.
municipal	Referring to an incorporated or chartered city or town.

municipal court   Lower court which usually tries criminal misdemeanors and civil matters where the amount in dispute is less than a certain, statutorily-established sum. A limited court.

muniments of title   Documentary evidence of title to real property.

murder   The intentional killing of a human being by a sane person, with malice aforethought.

music   Any artistically patterned combination of sounds.

musician   Person who performs music upon an instrument, or who is otherwise capable of producing music.

must   Shall. An imperative, mandatory command; without option or choice. Distinguishing between the mandatory "must" or "shall," and the permissive "may," is critical in interpreting contracts, orders, and statutes.

mutual   Referring to anything which both (or all) parties have or do in common.

N

name and likeness

Unique, identifiable attributes of a person, generally including the person's name, voice, likeness and biographical information. These so-called personality or publicity rights are protected against unauthorized commercial use under common law and, in some states, by statute (*e.g.*, California Civil Code § 3344.) Further, these rights have been held to be inheritable in most jurisdictions, and to accrue to the benefit of a deceased personality's estate.

Napoleonic Code

Code of laws formulated by the French emperor during his reign, relying solely on its written statutes as interpreted by judges on a case-by-case basis, rather than relying on the prior decisions of earlier cases. Distinct from the Common Law of England which underlies most American jurisprudence, a remnant of the Napoleonic Code continues to exist in the laws of Louisiana. (*Cf.*, "common law.")

National Labor Relations Board

Federal regulatory agency which conducts secret ballot elections among employees to determine if they wish to be represented in collective bargaining agreements (*i.e.*, become unionized), and which acts to prevent and/or remedy unfair labor practices. Generally referred to by its acronym, NLRB.

natural law

Standards of conduct derived solely from universal moral principles. A philosophical ideal.

natural person

A human being, as distinct from a corporation or other entity deemed a "person" for legal purposes.

naught

Zero. Nothing.

nebulous

Without concrete or certain form; cloudy, indistinct, uncertain or fluctuating.

necessary party	Person or entity whose rights or interests will be directly affected by the outcome of litigation, and who, to avoid injustice, must be joined as a party in the case and thereby allowed to appear and present argument and authority supporting such rights and interests. (See "indispensable party.")
necessary	That which is essential or unavoidable, rather than merely convenient or desirable.
necessary inference	Logical conclusion which must unavoidably follow a particular line of reasoning.
negative pregnant	A negative statement (denial) which implies an affirmative response (admission).
negligence	A breach of duty. Failure to exercise the due care toward others which a reasonable person understands and accepts as a common duty.
negligent	Careless or reckless in fulfilling responsibilities or duties, or failing to fulfil such responsibilities or duties.
negotiable instrument	Any writing which can be exchanged for value (cash), including, but not limited to, checks, promissory notes, bills of exchange, securities, and bonds.
negotiate (1)	To present an endorsed negotiable instrument (*e.g.,* a check) for its monetary value in exchange.
negotiate (2)	To engage in a bargaining process with one or more others, with the intention of arriving at mutually-acceptable terms of agreement (contract).
negotiation (1)	The exchange of a negotiable instrument for value.
negotiation (2)	Process of bargaining, with the intention of arriving at the final terms and conditions of a contract.

net	Amount of money or value remaining after all costs and expenses have been paid. Assets minus liabilities.

In entertainment contracts, this short, simple-appearing word can lead to a broad range of disputes.

The three elements for calculating "Net" are: *(a)* Income; *(b)* Costs; and *(c)* Expenses. Unless each of these is defined and limited by the contract terms, "net" may become subject to "creative accounting," with "income" narrowly construed, and "costs" and "expenses" broadly construed. (See "costs," "expenses," and "income." See also "creative accounting," "but not limited to," and "without limitation") |
net present value	Calculated fair market value of mid- to long-term asset. Discounted amount payable today for a long-term asset. Generally abbreviated NPV.
net price to dealer	See "Published Price to Dealer."
net worth	A calculated sum determined by subtracting the value of total liabilities from the value of total assets.
new matter	Facts or legal issues not previously known or available.
next of kin	One's nearest blood relative.
nil	Nothing. *(Latin)* Contraction of *nihil*, meaning nothing, naught, or zero.
NLRB	National Labor Relations Board
no contest	English translation of the plea, *nolo contendre*, meaning "I do (will) not contest it." A plea which may be entered by the defendant in criminal cases, effectively the same as "guilty" for the purposes of the criminal charge, but without effect in regard to any concurrent or subsequent civil suit regarding the same acts. (Conversely, a plea or verdict of "guilty" in a criminal matter relieves the plaintiff in a related civil case of its burden of proof upon the issue.)

no-par stock	Shares in a corporation which are issued without a par value being set.
nolo contendere	Literally, "I will not contest it." *(Latin)* (See "no contest.")
nom de plume	Pen name. *(French)* A pseudonym used by an author in lieu of his or her legal name.
nominal	In name only.
nominal damages	A small sum awarded to plaintiff in a lawsuit for "actual" damages, to lay a necessary legal foundation for a contemporaneous award of circumstantial, special, punitive, exemplary and/or other damages.
nominate	To designate a person, by name, to perform some agency, action, or office.
nominee	Person or entity who is named to act for another.
non compos mentis	Referring to one who is not of sound mind.
nonetheless	However; yet; notwithstanding; regardless; despite something to the contrary. Often used following a concession, to dilute or negate its effect. *E.g.,* "It's raining. Nonetheless, I'm going out."
nonfeasance	Failure to perform duties, tasks, or obligations required in the management of a business, public office, or other responsibility.
non sequitur	"It does not follow." *(Latin)* A statement, observation, or response which bears no apparent relationship to that which preceded it.

non- contestability clause	Insurance policy provision which limits the period of time during which the insurer can challenge the eligibility of the insured to have received coverage, after which the insurer must perform under the policy regardless of any irregularities (including fraudulent misrepresentation) in the original application.
non-contiguous	Referring to two or more parcels of real property which have no common point of boundary between them (*i.e.*, they do not touch upon each other at any place.) Non-adjacent.
non-discretionary trust	Trust wherein the trustee is instructed to make only certain, specified investments, and no others.
non-dramatic musical works	Musical works not created as part of an encompassing dramatic work. Single compositions from a dramatic work, when recorded separately from that dramatic work, are deemed nondramatic musical works. (See "grand right" and "small right.")
non-profit corporation	Organization incorporated under state laws and approved by taxing authorities as being a not-for-profit enterprise. Such corporations have no shareholders and declare no profits or dividends, but use their income to pay their operational costs and expenses, with the reminder used to perform such altruistic functions as are within their charter. Also referred to as a "not-for-profit corporation."
non-suit	Dismissal of lawsuit, at trial, upon showing that plaintiff has failed to introduce evidence to support each and all of the essential factual elements necessary to the causes of action pled.
nonrecoupable	Referring to a cost or expense which is not subject to recoupment from royalties. Non-recoverable expense.
nonreturnable	Referring to an advance which need not be repaid, even if subsequent royalties are insufficient to offset that advance.

normal retail channels	Phrase used to describe distribution for sale at full retail price, as distinct from distribution intended for discount sale. Often used in recording contracts to distinguish royalty-earning sales from non-royalty or reduced-royalty sales.
north of the versus	Colloquial term for plaintiff in a lawsuit. One whose name appears above the "*vs.*" on the title page of the complaint.
not guilty	Plea of a person who denies having committed crime(s) charged, or verdict of jury upon finding that the prosecution has not met its burden of proving guilt beyond a reasonable doubt.
not guilty by reason of insanity (or mental disease or defect)	Plea of person charged with crime who admits to the commission of such crime but denies criminal liability on the grounds of insanity. Verdict of jury affirming such plea. (See "insanity.") A person found not guilty by reason of insanity avoids a prison sentence, but is usually committed to a mental health facility for an indeterminate period, generally depending on a court finding that he or she is no longer a danger to him- or herself, or to others.
notary	(See "notary public")
notary public	Person authorized as a public officer of the state in which he or she resides to administer oaths, and to attest and certify, by his or her signature and official seal, the identity of signatories to legal documents, as well as performing other official functions. (See, "affidavit"; "acknowledgment" and "jurat.")
notice	(1) To become aware.
	(2) Communication which makes another aware of certain facts, circumstances, events, dates, impending action, and/or conditions.
	(3) In litigation, communication to adverse parties or their counsel, usually in writing, advising as to when and where a proceeding is to be held, and for what purpose.

notice of default	Notice to an obligated party that he, she, or it has failed to timely perform an obligation. In particular, a recordable notice sent to a borrower that mortgage payments have not been timely received, the recording of which notice is the first step toward initiating foreclosure. Usually abbreviated N.O.D.
notice provision	Portion of contract defining the manner in which formal notice must be given by one party to another in order to be deemed effective.
notice to quit	Notice given by landlord to tenant, demanding that premises be vacated by a certain date, at least a certain number of days from date of notice, as set by contract or by statute on a state-by-state basis. (*E.g.,* 30-, 60-, 90-Day Notice to Quit.)
notice to pay or quit	Conditional notice given by landlord to tenant, demanding that either rent be paid by a certain date, or that the premises be vacated by that certain date. Period between notice date and demanded pay-or-quit date are set by statute, on a state-by-state basis. (*E.g.,* 3-, 5-, 10-Day Notice to Pay or Quit.)
notice to perform or quit	Virtually identical to a notice to pay or quit, a notice to perform or quit demands that the tenant perform some covenant or obligation which is required under the terms of tenancy (lease) other than payment of rent. *E.g.,* abate excessive noise; not keep a pet, etc. Period between notice date and demanded perform-or-quit date are set by statute, on a state-by-state basis. (*E.g.,* 5-, 10-15-Day Notice to Perform Covenant or Quit.)
notwithstanding	Despite something to the contrary. Regardless. Used to acknowledge a fact while negating its effect. *E.g.,* "Rain notwithstanding, I'm going out."
NOV	"*Non obstante veredicto*" *(Latin)* Notwithstanding the verdict. Judgment entered by the Court for one party, despite a jury verdict for the other party.

novation	New agreement between parties to an earlier contract, which completely supercedes (replaces) all older contracts, making them void.
NPV	See "Net Present Value."
nugatory	That which is of no force nor effect. A legal nullity.
nuisance	A condition which arises from the unwarranted, unreasonable, or unlawful use by a person of his or her own property, which creates a material annoyance, obstruction, impediment or injury to the rights or person of another, or to the public.
nullity	That which has no force nor effect, and may be treated as non-existent.
nunc pro tunc	Literally, "now for then." *(Latin)* Refers to a court action which, while actually done on one date, is deemed to have taken effect as of an earlier, specified date.

O

oath

(1) A statement which attests that the person making it is and will be bound by conscience and/or by religious beliefs, to perform a duty fully, faithfully and truthfully. Oaths traditionally invoke a deity (*e.g.*, God) as witness to the oath. For those to whom such a statement is morally repugnant or religiously proscribed, an affirmation is a legally acceptable substitute for an oath.

(2) In court proceedings, an oath (or affirmation) is administered to each witness, who thereby swears (or affirms) that he or she will "tell the truth, the whole truth, and nothing but the truth" in the matter then before the Court.

obfuscate

To misdirect, confuse, cloud, or unnecessarily complicate an issue, through words or actions, in order to conceal or convolute the truth of the matter.

obfuscation

An action or thing which tends to confuse, cloud, or unnecessarily complicate an issue.

obfuscatory

Referring to that which tends to confuse, cloud, or unnecessarily complicate an issue.

obiter dictum

Literally, a remark made along the way. *(Latin)* Court's comment made within a ruling which is not essential to the decision stated or to that ruling. The plural is *obiter dicta*.

object

To take exception to; to protest. To request that the court not allow a particular question or introduction of particular evidence, on the ground that the question or the proffered evidence violates some specific legal rule of evidence.

objection

Protest regarding the legal propriety of a question, or the legal admissibility of proffered evidence.

obligation	Legal duty to do some particular thing, or to refrain from doing some particular thing.
obligatory	That which must be performed. Compulsory; mandatory; required.
obligee	Person to whom, or for whose benefit, an obligation is owed.
obligor	Person who is required to perform an obligation.
obo **o/b/o**	On behalf of. Used to indicate that the person signing a document is doing so as the agent of another person or entity.
obscene	Subjective reference to material held to be unfit for publication. Under a three-prong test established by the U. S. Supreme Court, "obscene" material is limited to a work which *(a)* depicts or describes "patently offensive" sexual conduct; ***and** (b)* which, looked at in its entirety and applying contemporary community standards, appeals to prurient interests (*i.e.,* is capable of arousing lust) in an average person, ***and** (c)* which, looked at in its entirety from the perspective of a reasonable person, applying a national standard, lacks serious artistic, literary, political or scientific value.
obscenity	That which is obscene.
obstruction of justice	Attempted or actual interference with the administration or proceedings of a court, or of a court officer in the performance of his or her duty.
obvious	Easily understood, discovered, or perceived. Patently clear.
occupancy	Possession and use of real property, either by an owner or by a tenant.
occupant	An owner or tenant who occupies real property.

occupation (1)	Possession, control, use of real property. State of occupancy.
occupation (2)	Profession, trade, craft, or vocation. Activity in which one is principally engaged, especially as a means of livelihood. That which one primarily does to make a living.
occupational hazard	Risk of injury, disease, or death which is unique to, inherent in, or heightened by reason of, one's particular occupation. (*E.g.,* Deafness is an occupational hazard of rock musicians.)
occupational disease	Illness which results from long-term exposure to conditions or substances which are common to one's occupation. (*E.g.,* Pneumoconiosis (black lung) is an occupational disease affecting coal miners.)
of counsel	Refers to an attorney who is not the principal attorney in a matter, or to an attorney who is affiliated with a particular law firm, but is not an associate, partner, member or employee of that firm.
of record	Those persons and things which have come before the court in the course of an action, such that they are identified in the court's records. An attorney who currently represents a party to an action is referred to as being "of record" or as the "attorney-of-record."
off calendar	Removal a previously scheduled matter from the court's docket. Cancellation by the court, either on its own initiative or at the request of a party, of a previously scheduled court appearance. Referring to a previously-scheduled proceeding which has been cancelled or postponed indefinitely (*i.e.,* without setting a new date.)
offense	A violation of criminal laws, whether felony or misdemeanor.
offer	Specific proposal to enter into an agreement with another upon specified terms.

offer and acceptance	Method by which a contract is created and becomes effective. Once an offer has been accepted, without conditions, and any consideration has been given in reliance, a contract exists as between the parties. (*Cf.*, "counteroffer")
offer of proof	Explanation made to the court during proceedings as to the expected substance and relevance of testimony or evidence which is not yet before the court.
offeree	One to whom an offer is made.
offeror	One who makes an offer to another.
officer	One who holds office and position of trust, authority and command, either within a corporation (*e.g.*, president, vice-president, *etc.*) or in government or military service.
official	That which has been done by virtue of an office. An authorized act, document, action, or event.
official misconduct	Unlawful and/or improper acts by a public official in violation of his or her oath of office.
offset	Deduction by a debtor of an amount claimed by the debtor to be owed to him or her by the creditor. See also, "setoff."
offshore	That which is done or which exists outside the United States, including its territories and possessions. Entities which are formed and exist, and transactions which occur, within and under the sovereignty of a nation other than the United States.
ombudsman	A semi-official position, empowered to hear individual grievances and to then advocate on behalf of the aggrieved before an otherwise-inaccessible higher authority.

omission	(1) Left out. Something which should have been included, but was not. An error of exclusion. (2) Failure to perform an agreed act, or an act which one is duty-bound to perform.
omnibus	Containing two or more independent matters. Frequently embodying a number of completely unrelated matters within a single whole. A catch-all.
on or before	Phrased used to designate a date which the last date upon which a specified act or obligation is to be performed, or (in pleading) the last date of an approximate period during which something is alleged to have occurred.
on the merits	Referring to a ruling or judgment which is made after the court has had an opportunity to review all relevant evidence.
on all fours	A legal issue which is substantially identical to a previous issue which had been the subject of a prior decision, so that the authority of that earlier opinion is directly relevant to the new issue in all salient respects.
on calendar	Referring to a proceeding which is scheduled to occur.
on demand	Provision stating that an obligation is to be performed when requested, rather than upon some particular date.
on file	Anything which has been formally to the clerk of the court and accepted for filing. (*Cf.,* "lodged" and "received.")
on or after	Phrased used to designate a date which the earliest date upon which a specified act or obligation is to be performed, or (in pleading) the earliest date of an approximate period during which something is alleged to have occurred.
on or around	Phrase referring to a date or locale which is approximate. Also written, "on or about." (See also "at or around" and "in or around.")

on spec　　　　　Purchase, investment, expenditure, advance of funds, or deferral of collection, made in anticipation of realizing future profit as a result. Literally, "speculative."

one stop　　　　Indirect distributor which buys albums in moderate quantity from a label or distributor, and then resells them in very small quantities to independent retailers, at a markup. One stops are often purchasers of "cutouts."

open court　　　Judicial proceedings which the general public may attend.

open-ended　　　Referring to a transaction or contract which does not have a fixed term, but which is complete when certain events have occurred, such as delivery of a certain number of recordings.

opening statement　Counsel's statement to the court, at the commencement of trial (or later) explaining everything that counsel expects to prove during the course of the trial.

operation of law　That which occurs by reason of a law, or a newly-enacted law.

operating agreement　Multi-party agreement between members of a limited liability company which sets forth and governs the nature and operations of that company. (*Cf.*, "bylaws.")

opinion　　　　　Detailed explanation of a court's ruling or judgment, setting forth an analysis of the facts and the legal reasoning and authority supporting the court's decision.

opinion letter　　Formal statement by an attorney, accountant, or other professional, stating his or her professional opinion in regard to a particular matter. In some instances, an opinion letter may be statutorily required as a condition for certain transactions. (*E.g.*, an attorney's opinion letter may be necessary to obtain permission to offer certain securities for sale.)

option	That which one may choose to do or to not do. An agreement, or a provision within a contract, which sets forth conditions under which a party to the agreement has the right to do or to not do some particular thing, or to require the other party to do or to not do some particular thing.
or	As with "and," the common conjunction "or" can be of immense significance in construing contracts and statutes. "Or" expressly embodies a choice between two or more provisions, where one (but not both) are operative or executory.
O.R.	Acronym for "own recognizance," referring to the release of a criminal defendant from custody without the posting of bail, upon the court's perception that the defendant's own conscience and sense of duty is sufficient assurance that he or she will appear for further proceedings. (Also abbreviated as "R.O.R." for "released [on his or her] own recognizance.")
oral contract	Agreement made in spoken words, without reducing them to a writing. Colloquially an oral contract is frequently referred to as a "verbal" contract, however written contracts are also "verbal." (*Cf.*, "verbal contract")
ORAP	Acronym for "Order to Appear." Court order compelling a person over whom the Court has *in personam* jurisdiction to appear at a particular time and place. Frequently, it is used to compel the attendance of a judgment debtor so that he or she may be questioned as to assets, income, and other relevant matters in an attempt to obtain payment of the judgment debt.
order	(1) Authoritative command, instruction, or direction. Any instruction given or requirement imposed by a judge, regardless of whether written or spoken.
	(2) Request that something to be manufactured, provided, or delivered.
	(3) Systematic arrangement on the basis of pragmatic, esthetic, philosophical, or harmonic principles.

order of argument	In arguing before the court, the moving or initiating party presents its argument, then the opposing party presents its response. The original party is then permitted to argue again, in reply to that response. If the reply introduces new matter, the opposing party may be permitted a rebuttal, and the originating party a surrebuttal, to address that new matter.
order shortening time	Court order, made upon a party's motion or *sua sponte*, reducing the statutory amount of time which is usually afforded to perform some act. Thus a motion which might normally require three week's notice before hearing could be heard sooner, with the dates for filing an opposition and a reply reduced accordingly. Such order is generally referred to as an "OST."
order to show cause	More fully, an "Order to Appear and Show Cause," is issued *sua sponte* or on the motion of a party, setting forth a prospective action which the Court intends to take unless the affected parties can appear at a specified place and time to then and there demonstrate to the Court's satisfaction that good cause exists for the court to <u>not</u> take the proposed action. (Usually abbreviated as "O.S.C." or "OSC")
ordinance	A statute enacted by a county, city, or town.
ordinary	Regular, customary and usual.
ordinary course of business	Those events and transactions which are of a kind that can reasonably be expected to occur within the normal and usual scope of a business' regular operations. Those things which are customarily a regular part of the operations of a particular business or type of business.
original jurisdiction	Authority of a court to accept the initial filing of particular action, based on a provision of law which establishes that such court is a proper forum for that case to be tried.

OSC	Acronym for "Order to [Appear and] Show Cause." Court order, issued *sua sponte* or on the motion of a party, which sets forth a prospective action which the Court intends to take unless the affected parties can appear at a specified place and time and demonstrate to the Court's satisfaction that good cause exists sufficient to dissuade the court from taking such proposed action.
OSHA	Acronym for "Occupational Safety and Health Administration." Federal agency which sets, administers and enforces workplace safety standards. Each state also has its own agency which may be known by a different name, but which performs similar regulatory and enforcement functions.
OST	Acronym for "Order Shortening Time."
ostensible	That which has all the superficial indications of being something which it may, in fact, not be.
ostensible agent	Person who has the appearance of being an employee or authorized representative or another, under circumstances which would lead a reasonable person to believe that such authority exists. An ostensible agent may, as a matter of law, be deemed a "real" agent, by reason of the principal's conduct in regard to such person.
ostensible authority	Apparent authority to do something or represent another person or entity. (See "ostensible agent")
oust	To put out; eject. To terminate another's occupancy, possession, or enjoyment of a property, position, interest, or right.
out of court	Referring to negotiations, settlements and other exchanges between parties either without resort to litigation, or conducted during litigation but separate and apart from it.
out-of-pocket expenses	Money actually paid for reasonably necessary items in the performance of some project or employment.

outlaw	Generally, a criminal. One who habitually acts in violation of law or social custom.
overdub	Process of recording additional material on top of an existing recording to enhancing or expand that prior recording.
overrule	To deny or disapprove an evidentiary objection or certain types of motions. (*E.g.,* a demurrer is sustained or overruled, rather than granted or denied.) (See, "sustain.")
overt act	Action which might be innocent, in and of itself, but which is manifestly part of a criminal plan.
owe	Having a legal duty to pay funds due to another.
own	Having legal title or right to property, beyond mere possession, custody, or control.
own recognizance	The release of a criminal defendant from custody without the posting of bail, upon the court's perception that the defendant's own conscience and sense of duty is sufficient assurance that he or she will appear for further proceedings. Generally abbreviated "O.R." or "R.O.R."
owner	One who has legal title or right to property, beyond mere possession, custody, or control.
ownership	The legal relationship of an owner to property, with the right to convey that relationship to another. Ownership is distinguishable from possession, custody or control.

P

p.	Standard abbreviation for "page," it is usually pluralized by doubling (*i.e.*, "pp.," for "pages.")
℗	Symbol for registered copyright in a sound recording. Generally referred to as a "circle-p," the letter "p" stands for "phonorecord."
π	Greek letter "pi." Used as attorney's shorthand notation for "plaintiff." *Cf.,* "Δ" ("delta.")
¶	Standard typographical symbol for "paragraph," it is pluralized by doubling (*i.e.,* "¶¶" for "paragraphs.") The symbol is also occasionally used as an alternative attorney's shorthand notation for "plaintiff."
P&A's	See "points and authorities."
P/L	Profit and Loss. Also alternatively written as "P&L." See "Income Statement."
packaging	Practice of assembling key personnel for an entertainment project, frequently obtaining all or most of them from people previously affiliated with or represented by the agency packaging the project. See "commitment letter."
packaging charge	A percentage or fixed sum deducted from the retail price (SRLP) of a recording, before calculating artist's royalties, on the theory that physical elements of the final product are not derived from the artist's creative work. Also referred to as a "container" charge or fee. Generally, the packaging charge is 25% of the SRLP. See also, "container charge."
par	(1) The face value of a stock or bond; (2) On an equal level. Average.

paralegal	Specially trained non-attorney who performs routine tasks requiring knowledge of the law, at the direction of an attorney.
paramount title	A right to property which is held to be superior and which prevails over any other claim of right to that property.
pardon	An official forgiveness for a crime, granted to an accused or convicted offender by the executive authority of a state governor (for state crimes) or the President (for federal crimes), barring all further prosecution or punishment the offender for the pardoned acts. See also, "clemency."
parent	(1) Natural or adoptive father or mother of a person. (2) A business entity which owns a subsidiary company, of which subsidiary it is the parent. Hence, "parent corporation."
pari delicto	Equally at fault. Legal doctrine stating that court's will not enforce an invalid contract and that no party can recover in an action reliant upon an illegal contract.
pari passu	In equal amounts. Without preference. Distribution to all entitled parties not in proportion to their respective entitlement, but rather in equal sums, dollar for dollar, until each has received their respective payment in full. (*Cf.,* "pro rata") In groups where the percentages are varied due to differing levels of contribution, a *pari passu* agreement – usually up to a certain initial aggregate income – can avoid friction between members, since each initially receives identical amounts
parish	(1) In Louisiana, a local governmental area equivalent to a county in other states. (See, "Napoleonic Code") (2) The geographic area served by a particular church.

partial performance	The doing of some portion, but less than all, of the obligations of a contract. Partial performance, either before or after a breach of the contract, when expressly accepted by the other party, in writing, as full satisfaction, extinguishes any remaining obligations. (See "accord and satisfaction.") Also, partial performance is an affirmative defense to a cause of action for rescission.
parody	Humorous, satirical and/or editorial work derived from an existing song, play, writing, or other work of art. (See "fair use.")
parol	Speech; A spoken statement, as opposed to a statement made in writing.
parol contract	An oral contract.
parol evidence	Oral evidence; testimony.
parol evidence rule	Judicial rule of evidence which generally prohibits oral testimony as to the contents of a written document, on the ground that the document speaks for itself. The rule does not forbid oral testimony which is consistent with a reasonable interpretation of the terms of the writing.
parole	Release of a convicted criminal defendant after he or she has served a portion of his or her sentence, upon terms and conditions which the convict promises to honor. Parole is a special form of promise which, although made under duress, is nonetheless binding.
partial	Incomplete. Less than complete or whole.
participate	To invest, with others, in a business or venture.

partition	Cause of action in which a co-owner of real or personal property seeks a court determination as to the respective rights of all co-owners, and a distribution of the fair, proportional value to each co-owner of their respective share, usually through court-ordered liquidation of the property. Partition is the usual remedy when partners cannot amicably settle a dispute between them as to their respective rights and interests in their common business.
partner	One of two or more persons who co-own a business or property in common with each other. (See, "general partner")
partnership	A business enterprise owned by two or more individuals (partners.) In this most basic form, it is more properly referred to a "general partnership" to distinguish it from more complex forms of partnership, such as limited partnerships and limited liability partnerships. (See, "limited liability partnership" and "limited partnership." See also, "corporation," "limited liability company")
party	(1) Any of the named participants in a lawsuit or other legal proceeding. (See, "litigant.") (2) Any of the persons or entities who enter into a contract and are bound to perform some obligation under that contract.
party of the first part	Phrase used in some written contracts as a subsequent reference to the individual or entity first identified in the contract. Generally, at the point where the intended party's true name is first recited, there will be a reference stating, in effect, "hereinafter 'Party of the First Part.'"
party of the second part	Phrase used in some written contracts as a subsequent reference to the individual or entity identified second in the contract.
party of the third [etc.] part	Phrase used in some written, multiple-party contracts as a subsequent reference to the individual or entity identified third (or forth, fifth, etc.) in the contract.

passenger	(1) One who has paid a fare (*i.e.,* purchased passage) to ride on a commercial vehicle, including airplanes, ships, trains, buses, taxis, coaches, rickshaws, etc., over the operation of which the passenger has no control. (2) Anyone within a vehicle who is not in operational control of that vehicle.
passive	That which takes no action. (*E.g.,* a "passive investor" is one who entrusts his money to a broker or business and thereafter takes no active part in determining how that money will be utilized.)
patent (1)	Obvious. Clear. Manifest. Unquestionable. Obvious. Patent facts are those which no one is likely to suggest are anything other than factual.
patent (2)	Generally, any grant by government authority of some privilege, property or authority. More commonly, a "patent" refers to a legal monopoly granted for a limited time, by government license, for an innovative work of creative invention or improvement. Literary and artistic works are not patentable, but may be protected similarly through copyright.
patent ambiguity	Language appearing within a writing which creates an unavoidable paradox or confusion as to its intended meaning. (*E.g.,* "This provision shall remain in full force and effect only for so long as it has neither force nor effect and at no other time.")
patent defect	Flaw in a product, property, or document which is clearly obvious upon reasonable inspection, without requiring specialized knowledge or tests. (*Cf.,* "latent defect.")
patent infringement	Unlawful manufacture and/or use of a patented invention or improvement, without permission of the patent owner.

patent pending	A work of invention or improvement for which an application for patent has been filed and preliminarily approved. Frequently abbreviated to "pat. pending" or "pat. pend." an item may be made available for sale bearing that notice, with all of the protections afforded by patent law.
pauper	Person so poor as to be unable to provide himself or herself with the necessities of life and so must be supported at the public expense. (See, "*in forma pauperis.*")
pawn	(1) Pledge of an item of personal property as security for a loan. (See "bailment.") (2) One whose actions are controlled or manipulated by another, for that other's purposes or benefit.
pay	(1) To deliver money owed. (2) Colloquially, the money one receives for services. Salary.
pay to play	Arrangement between venue and performer, in which performer pays or guarantees a certain minimum amount to the venue, and then receives some or all of the fees being charged for admission to the performance. Frequently, the performers will purchase a minimum number of admission tickets from the venue, in advance, and then sell or otherwise distribute them.
payable	Referring to an owed debt which has become due. (See "accounts payable.")
payable on demand	A debt which must be paid immediately upon the formal request of the person to whom it is owed.
payee	Person or entity to whom or which payment is made. The person or entity named on the face of a check following the words "Pay to the order of..."
payment in full	Payment of a sum representing an entire obligation, leaving nothing owing.

payola	Colloquial term for the unlawful practice of providing monetary payments, gifts, or other items of value to disc-jockeys, programmers, station managers or others capable of influencing airplay, as an inducement to have a particular label's or artist's recordings receive preferential treatment in broadcasting.
payor	Person or entity who or which makes a payment to another. The person or entity against whose account a check is issued and from which account the funds to pay that check will be deducted.
pecuniary	Relating to money.
peer	An equal. One of equal rank and station in life. In a nominally classless society, all individuals of sound mind and legal age are considered to be "peers" of each other. In monarchies, "peer" generally refers to a member of the nobility or ruling class.
peer review	Scrutiny, analysis and evaluation of a professional's work, and particularly his or her published opinions, theories and conclusions, by other members of that same profession, seeking to validate or invalidate that work according to that profession's generally accepted standards.
penal	Referring to crime and/or punishment.
penalty	Imposed consequence for wrongful conduct, including one or more of: private censure, public humiliation, monetary fine, loss of privilege, forfeiture of rights, imposed term of service, restrictions, imprisonment or death.
penalty clause	Contract provision which establishes pre-agreed consequences for non-performance or untimely performance of a contractual obligation. (See "penalty" and "liquidated damages.")

pendent jurisdiction	Federal policy which permits a federal court to try state-law-based causes of action, applying state law, where those state law causes of action are part of a complaint properly filed in federal court and over which the federal court has jurisdiction. (*E.g.,* In a federal civil rights case where the complaint also includes a separate cause of action for trespass, the federal court will try the entire case, applying federal law to the federal (civil rights) cause of action and state law to the state law (trespass) cause of action.)
pendente lite	Literally, "awaiting the suit." *(Latin)* Refers to occurrences during the course of litigation, from filing through conclusion.
penitent	Expressing remorse. Also, the person expressing such remorse, or a person conferring privately with a clergyman.
per	Latin preposition meaning "by means of" or "by." Often used alone to indicate "by the instruction of" or "in accordance with."
per capita	Literally, "by head," *(Latin)* refers to any matter determined according to the number of individuals or households.
per capita **income**	The annual earnings of an (average) individual or household within a particular defined area, which may be based on geography, profession, age group, or other criteria.
per curiam	Literally, "by the court." *(Latin)* Refers to an opinion of an entire court, rather than a majority opinion prepared by only one judge.
per diem	Literally, "by the day." *(Latin)* Generally refers to a daily allowance for costs or expenses, paid in addition to earned salary.
per se	Literally, "by itself" or "by himself." *(Latin)* Inherently. Without the need for anything else. Taken alone.

percipient	Having knowledge by reason of direct perception, as with an eyewitness.
peremptory	Absolute, final, decisive; not subject to delay or reconsideration.
peremptory challenge	The right of the parties in a jury trial to summarily discharge a potential juror. Such challenges are limited by court rule or order to only a certain number for each side. While a peremptory challenge can be for no particular reason, it cannot be for an <u>improper</u> reason, such as to exclude a particular ethic group from the jury.
perfect	To complete; to finalize; to conclude all elements required to assure full legal force and effect.
perfected	That which has had all necessary legal steps concluded and is now of full force and effect. *E.g.:* Title to real property is perfected when an executed and notarized deed has been recorded in the Office of the County Recorder.
perform	(1) To fulfill legal obligations required under a contract. (2) To comply with a court order or directive. (3) To present oneself before others for their entertainment.
performance fees	Fees earned for public performance of a copyrighted recording, generally collected and disbursed by a performing rights society, such as ASCAP, BMI or SESAC.
perks	See "perquisites."
performance	(1) Fulfillment of contract obligations. (2) An entertainment.

performing rights organization	Any one of several organizations which collect fees and royalties on behalf of their members for public performance and commercial broadcast use of their members' copyrighted works. (See "ASCAP," "BMI," "SESAC" and "SOCAN")
perjurer	One who intentionally lies under oath, or in a declaration voluntarily executed under penalty of perjury.
perjury	Crime of intentionally lying after having taken an oath to tell the truth, or in a declaration voluntarily executed under penalty of perjury.
permanent injunction	Court order (decree) which forever prohibits certain action or inaction. (See "preliminary injunction.")
permissive	Allowed, but not required. Refers to any act which may be done, as distinct from an act which must be done and from an act which is forbidden to be done.
permit	To allow, whether by express consent or licence, or by acquiescence (through silence or inaction).
perpetuity	Unending; forever; without termination.
perquisites	Benefits or privileges claimed as though a matter of right. Additional benefits which one expects to receive, beyond salary or wages. Often contracted to "perqs" or (misspelled) "perks."
person	A human being or certain recognized forms of legal entity (*e.g.*, corporations, limited liability companies) which are regarded as "persons" for legal purposes.

personal manager	One who undertakes to oversee the career of a performer or group, usually for a percentage of income received either as a direct result of his or her efforts, or at any time during the term of the management contract, depending upon the negotiated terms of such contract. A personal manager's authority to act on behalf of an artist or group is based in contract, and may be narrowly constrained, or broadly granted, depending upon the terms of that contract and of any power of attorney contained in that agreement. (See also, "agent," "manager," "power of attorney," and "sunset clause." *Cf.*, "business manager.")
personal property	All property which is not "real property."
personal service	Delivery of legal documents directly into the hands of an affected party, or directly into the hands of an agent of such party who is legally designated and required to accept such service.
personal services	Those marketable skills, talents, or qualities which are unusual or unique to an individual, and which may be provided to another, for consideration, under a contract.
personality	See "name and likeness."
personalty	Shortened form of the term "personal property." Chattels; any property which is not real property, including intangible property.
petit jury	A jury which is empaneled to hear a trial, as distinct from a "grand jury." See, "jury."
petition	Formal written request addressed to a court or other governmental officer or body, or to some other authority, seeking some particular redress, relief or action from that authority.

petty larceny	Petty theft. Illegal taking of a small amount of property or money. Petty larceny (petty theft) is distinguished from grand larceny (grand theft) based on the value and/or specific nature of that which is stolen, both of which are established by statute on a state-by-state basis. (*E.g.*, Petty theft may be taking of that which has a value of less than $400., but the theft of a horse worth less than $400 may nonetheless be charged as grand theft in some jurisdictions.)
phonorecord	In copyright matters, phonorecord refers to any physical object (*e.g.*, a vinyl record, a compact disc, a cassette tape, etc.) which is capable of preserving recorded sounds in a distributable form which permits those sounds to be reproduced and heard, usually through the use of some machine or device. Any object capable of preserving recorded sounds, particularly music. Record companies generally take the inevitability of new technology into account by including the phrase, "all media, whether now known or unknown" in their contracts.
	While all phonorecords are recordings, not all recordings are "phonorecords" for copyright purposes. The distinction can be critical, since the distribution of a "phonorecord" triggers the availability of compulsory licenses under the Copyright Act. (*Cf.*, "demo.")
picket	To demonstrate by standing or parading, and usually by carrying signs or banners, near a business, government office, or other facility, in protest or in favor of some cause.
pierce the corporate veil	To demonstrate that a corporation or other limited-liability entity lacks true independent existence, and serves merely as a conduit for its owners' assets, and as shield intended to protect its owners from liability. Upon satisfactory proof, the court may find those owners to be personally liable, and not shielded by the corporation. Failure to comply with corporate formalities, commingling of assets and liabilities, and/or lack of adequate capitalization, may be grounds for piercing the corporate veil.

pilferage	Theft, generally of small items from a business' inventory, supplies, or from shipments, frequently by employees.
pink slip	(1) Colloquial term for title document showing ownership of a vehicle; (2) Colloquial term for a notice of termination of employment.
pipeline	Referring to royalties or other monies which have been collected but which have not yet been paid or are not yet due to be paid.
piracy	Infringement through unauthorized copying and/or distribution of copyrighted works. Technically, piracy is the crime of robbery of ships or boats on the ocean.
pka (p/k/a, p.k.a.)	Acronym for "professionally known as." A professional stage name used by a performer, in lieu of his or her real name. In entertainment contracts, it is common to use the artist's legal name followed by "pka" and his or her professional name. *E.g.:* "John Jones and Sam Smith pka 'The Wankers.'"
plagiarism	Unlawful copying of significant parts of the writings or literary concepts of another, coupled with a subsequent false presentation or publication of the resulting derived work as being an original work of one's own independent creation. See also, "infringement."
plain error	Obvious mistakes made or permitted by the court at trial which clearly, substantially and prejudicially affected the rights of the accused. Such mistakes may be grounds for reversal or remand by the court of appeal, even if no timely objection was made at the time of trial, because refusal to do so would be an affront to the integrity and reputation of the judicial process.

plain view doctrine	Doctrine which provides that incriminating objects which are readily visible to a law enforcement officer, at a time and under circumstances where the officer has a lawful and legitimate right to be situated so as to see such objects, may be seized by the officer, without warrant, and subsequently introduced into evidence.
plaintiff	Party who initiates a lawsuit by filing a complaint with the court. A complainant. In attorneys' shorthand, the word "plaintiff" is usually abbreviated by using the Greek letter π (pi) or the typographical symbol ¶ (paragraph).
play or pay clause	Contract provision which requires that liquidated damages (monetary penalties) be paid by or on behalf of a performer in the event that no performance is given when scheduled or requested.
plea	In criminal law, the response by an accused defendant to the charges preferred against him or her. Normally, the plea will be either "guilty," "not guilty," or "*nolo contendre*" (*i.e.,* no contest).
plea in abatement	In civil proceedings, a responsive pleading, in lieu of answer, by which a defendant may challenge plaintiff's complaint not on the its merits or on grounds of jurisdiction or legal sufficiency, but rather upon the place, mode, or time of plaintiff's action. If sustained by the court, a plea in abatement merely postpones or suspends the proceedings for a time, while preserving all of plaintiff's rights.
plead	To prepare and file with the court any writing (pleading). The past tense can be either "pleaded" or "pled."
pleading	Any legal document filed in a court action.
pledge	To deposit personal property as security for a loan. (See also "bailment." and "pawn.")

plenary	Full; complete; entire. A comprehensive proceeding or session; full and complete; covering all matters; conducted by and of the whole.
plurality	The largest number out of a larger number. *Example:* In elections where none of multiple candidates receive a majority (more than half) of the votes cast, the winning candidate is the one who received more votes than any other. That winning candidate is said to have won by a plurality of votes.
PO	Acronym for "purchase order."
POA	Acronym for "Power of Attorney," used to denote that capacity in executing a document on behalf of another. See "power of attorney."
point	One percent (1%). There is a key distinction between "net" points (which may ultimately prove of little value), "gross" points which have maximum value. A definition of the basis upon which points are to be calculated is critical to determining their value.
points and authorities	Legal brief, outlining specific arguments and supporting those arguments by citation of statutory and case law relevant to the issue under consideration. Usually abbreviated as "P&A's"
poison pill	A provision inserted into an agreement, as a tactical measure, which when implemented has a devastating effect upon one or more of the contracting parties. Generally, such a provision is inserted into employment or other agreements, to dissuade prospective company takeover bids by automatically devaluing the company.
polygraph	A so-called "lie detector." A device which measures physiological changes in a witness, during questioning, which are then interpreted by an expert who may state his or her opinion as to the truthfulness of the responses given.

pornography	Words or images of sexual activity. Material that depicts erotic behavior and is intended to cause sexual excitement. While all that is "obscene" is pornographic, not all pornography is obscene. (See "obscenity.")
POS (1)	Acronym for "Point of Sale," referring to the place and time when a product is obtained by the ultimate consumer.
POS (2)	Acronym for "Proof Of Service." Also abbreviated "P/S."
posse comitatus	Literally, "possible force," *(Latin)* refers to the entire adult populace which governmental authority may draw upon, at need, for assistance in keeping the peace or enforcing the law. In the United States, the "Posse Comitatus Act" (18 USC § 1385) prohibits the Armed Forces from domestic law enforcement, except in special, limited, expressly authorized circumstances.
possess	To personally occupy or to have within one's personal and physical control. One may lawfully posses that which one owns, or unlawfully possess the property of another.
possession	Any item, object, property or asset over which one has physical control and/or custody. In possession: the condition of physically holding or controlling something.
possessory interest	The lawful right to posses, occupy, use, have, or control property, even without an ownership interest. *E.g.,* the lawful tenant has a possessory interest in the real property of another.

post (1)	(1) To affix a notice (*e.g.,* a warning of hazard, or a notice of legal proceedings) in a prominent and visible location, usually upon a door, gate or similar location such that persons entering are likely to see it.
	(2) To make an accounting entry, as in a ledger or financial journal, creating a record of a particular transaction.
	(3) Mail. (Unusual in U.S., but common in U.K.)
post (2)	Abbreviated form of "post-production."
post mortem	Literally, "after death," a medical examination of a body to determine cause of death or, (colloquially) any examination or analysis of an event after the fact.
postage	Fee charged for the delivery of mail, usually in the form of stamps sold for the purpose of being affixed to such mail, or by use of metered devices which imprint the amount of postage on the item being mailed. In some instances, failure to fully prepay required postage may invalidate legal service or notice.
postdated check	Check written and delivered, but with a date which is in the future, with the understanding that the check will not be negotiated (*i.e.,* cashed or deposited) until such later date. (See "conditional delivery.")
post-production	Those processes and activities necessary to completion of a music, film or video project following recording or filming (*e.g.,* sweetening, re-mixing, editing, *etc.*) to prepare the project for commercial release.
power	Authority to take action coupled with ability and means to accomplish that action.

power of attorney	Written document by which a person may legally authorize another to act for him or her in regard to certain particular matters (a limited power of attorney) or in regard to all matters (a general power of attorney.) The person giving the power of attorney is referred to as the "principal," and the person who is empowered to act for him or her is referred to as the "attorney-in-fact." The principal is legally bound by his or her attorney-in-fact's actions, as though the principal had personally acted.
PPD	Acronym for "Published Price to Dealers" *or* "Published Dealer Price." Wholesale price. Term used in foreign markets instead of "wholesale." The term "Base Price to Dealers" ("BPD") is also used interchangeably with "PPD." Basis for calculation of artist's royalties outside the U.S. and Canada.
PPM	Acronym for "Private Placement Memorandum." [Note: "ppm" (lower case) is the abbreviation for "parts per million."]
practicable	That which can likely be accomplished through available means.
practice	Regular habit, custom or usage.
pray	To make a request of the court for some form of relief or redress.
prayer	The concluding portion of a pleading which specifies the particular relief which is being sought.
precedent	That which has gone before. The published decision of a court adjudicating similar legal issues in an earlier case.
preclude	To prevent or prohibit. To exclude something, in advance.
preclusion	A forbidding of certain evidence, issues, or other matters from being later introduced. (*Cf.*, "exclusion")

preemption	A taking over or taking away of something. Assuming control. Doctrine that certain matters are of such national (rather than state or local) nature that they must be resolved under federal laws. Any state law on the issue is therefore superceded (preempted) and the matter must adjudicated under federal law. Under the preemption doctrine, the states may not make any law which is inconsistent with federal law. (See also, "supremacy clause.")
preference	A more-favored position. That which is done for the benefit of some, but not all, of those who are otherwise similarly situated. (*E.g.,* to pay one creditor, while not paying other creditors who are also owed money for similar goods or services.) Some preferences are required (*e.g.,* employee wages are to be paid before other creditors), while others may be forbidden. (*e.g.,* paying employees differently for identical work, on the basis of unlawful criteria.)
preferred stock	A class of shares in a corporation which entitles the holders to priority in receiving income from their shares before the holders of non-preferred (common) stock.
prejudice	A bias in favor of or against a party. Predisposition toward judgment in favor of one party, or against the other party, before considering all evidence. Lack of impartiality.
prejudicial	That which encourages or supports prejudice, bias, or lack of impartiality toward one party or against another party, before all evidence has been considered.
preliminary hearing	In criminal proceedings where there has been no Grand Jury indictment, a court hearing (without jury) to determine if there is a sufficient quantity of evidence to proceed to trial.
preliminary injunction	Court order, issued on a party's motion, after a complaint has been filed and before trial, which compels another party to do something, or to refrain from doing something, during the remaining period of the litigation. (See also, "permanent injunction.")

premeditation	Forming a conscious intention to do something. Planning, plotting or deliberating before acting.
premises	(1) The facts and circumstances which are before the court in a lawsuit. Those matters which a court may consider in making a ruling. (2) An occupied building, or demised portion of a building. (3) Real property, including the land and all improvements and appurtenances.
premium	(1) Reward or bonus for an act performed. (2) Payment made in consideration of insurance coverage. (3) That which is of a better or best quality.
prenuptial agreement	See "antenuptial agreement."
preponderance of evidence	Lowest of three standards of proof, the preponderance test applies only in civil matters and requires a determination as to whether, on balance, the evidence presented by one party is more or less convincing that the evidence presented by an adverse party with respect to an issue. If the balance is effectively even, the presumption is made against the party which has the burden of proof upon that issue.
president	The chief executive officer (CEO) of a corporation or other organization.
presiding judge	Judge who, within a particular courthouse or district, handles administrative matters for the court, usually including assignment of judges to particular cases, the hiring and firing of court personnel, and general oversight of court and clerical operations within the courthouse. Certain matters, particularly with respect to judicial conduct and jurisdictional challenges, are often heard by the presiding judge.
presumption	Fact which a court is legally required to assume to be true upon the basis of underlying conditions or facts.

presumption of innocence	Basic and fundamental protection afforded any person accused of a crime. Thus, a criminal defendant need not prove innocence, but rather it is the prosecution's burden to overcome the presumption of innocence by clear and convincing evidence, beyond a reasonable doubt. (See "burden of proof," "rebuttable presumption," and "standards of proof.")
pretrial	All matters which occur in the course of litigation, prior to the commencement of trial.
prevailing party	That party to a dispute who is adjudged to be the "winner." In contracts, attorney's fees clauses generally provide that the "prevailing party" is entitled to receive his or her attorney's fees.
price fixing	Crime of collusion, in which ostensible competitors agree to prices they will charge for their competing products, either to drive out other competitors, or to enhance profits, by an artificial retail price. Violation of the federal Sherman Anti-Trust Act.
prima facie	Literally, "at first look." *(Latin)* That which appears to be true from general appearances.
prima facie **case**	A cause of action or criminal charge in which all of the essential elements have been alleged and appear to have evidentiary support sufficient to prevail unless contradicted by other evidence.
principal	(1) In a loan, the actual amount lent. An original amount owed, exclusive of interest or other added charges. (2) The person on whose behalf an agent acts. (3) An actual participant in some action or endeavor.
principal place of business	That location where the largest portion of the operational activities of an enterprise are conducted.

prior inconsistent statement	Statement made by a witness at an earlier time which is contrary to subsequent testimony, introduced for the purpose of attacking credibility. Testimony as to a prior inconsistent statement is one of the exceptions to the hearsay rule.
prior restraint	Constitutionally-prohibited attempt to prevent publication of material before it is published. Prior restraint is permissible only in certain exceptional circumstances: (1) where the publication would present a "clear and present danger" to the country; (2) where the publication is "obscene"; or (3) where the publication would invade a zone of personal privacy.
priority	Right or privilege of being first, or ahead of others, usually in regard to scheduling of time.
privacy	Right to be free of invasive or unnecessary scrutiny; to be left alone and unmolested. Generic term for body of rights held to be inherent to each individual in a free society, said to exist only to the extent and for so long as it does not impinge upon the rights of others.
private carrier	Person or entity which, as a business, provides transportation or delivery services.
private placement memorandum	A type of security offering which is not federally regulated, by which an enterprise may solicit qualified investors. Private placement memoranda require careful compliance with applicable state Blue Sky Laws to avoid illegal solicitation, and are lawful only in certain limited circumstances. (See "Blue Sky Laws" and "prospectus.")
private property	Property owned by a legal person or persons.
privilege	A special benefit, exemption, immunity, or franchise granted to a person or to class of persons.

privileged communication	Statements and conversations made under circumstances of a professional or other relationship to which the law ascribes a privilege of secrecy, such that the no portion of the communication can be divulged except upon waiver of the privilege by the protected person. (*E.g.,* communications between attorney and client, or between priest and penitent.)
privity	Connection; contact; common relationship or interest between parties.
PRLA	"Phonograph Record Labor Agreement." Former master agreement between the AFM and record labels, the PRLA was renamed the Sound Recording Labor Agreement (SRLA) in 2002. Older recording contracts may still refer to PRLA in conjunction with union fund contributions.
pro bono	Literally, "for the good" *(Latin)*, is the shortened form of "*pro bono publico,*" ("for the public good") and refers to services that are provided as a public service, without expectation of payment.
pro forma	"As a matter of form," *(Latin)* refers to those formalities which are either required or which facilitate a process, although adding no material element to the matter at hand.
pro hac vice	Literally, "this time only," *(Latin)* refers to procedure by which an attorney licensed in one jurisdiction may be permitted to appear in another jurisdiction, without being formally admitted to the bar in that jurisdiction.
pro per	Abbreviated form of "*propria persona.*" (See, "*in pro per.*" and "*pro se.*")
pro rata	In proportion. Apportioned in accordance with percentages of interest or obligation. (*Cf.,* "*pari passu.*")
pro se	Literally "for himself." *(Latin)* Refers to a party who appears for himself or herself in a lawsuit, without an attorney.

pro tanto	Literally, "only to that extent." *(Latin).* Partial. Generally found in partial releases, where the underlying claim is excused only by so much as is received in partial consideration, and not in its entirety.
pro tem	Abbreviated form of *"pro tempore,"* (for the time being). Temporary. A temporary substitute.
pro tempore	See *"pro tem."*
probable cause	A good and legally sufficient reason to take or authorize further action.
probate	The process of adjudicating a will or trust, including appointment of trustees or administrators, and distribution of assets to creditors, heirs and beneficiaries. A specialized area of law, and a type of court, which deals with wills and trusts.
probation	A form of judicial clemency, in which person convicted of a lesser crime is permitted to remain at liberty, subject to certain terms and conditions which, if violated, may lead to the full sentence being imposed. A period during which one's behavior is scrutinized, as a determining factor for some later decision about that person.
probative	Anything that tends to prove something. Substantive evidence.
probative value	That quality of evidence which shows it to be relevant and useful in proving or disproving a matter at-issue in a case.
procedure	Methods, systems, protocols and administrative rules which guide all aspects of the judicial system.
proceeding	In broad terms, anything that is done in the course of litigation which is procedurally authorized, including filings, discovery, hearings, trial, judgment, appeal, etc.

process	Legal means (*i.e.,* writing) by which jurisdiction is established over a person or thing, or by which formal notice is given, upon service of the process. (*E.g.,* summons; subpoena; notice of levy, etc.)
process server	Person who serves legal papers, by delivering them into the hands of the person to whom they are directed, or by authorized. alternative means of delivery.
producer	Person responsible for all phases of the process of converting a creative concept into a final commercial product through selection, oversight, and final approval of all elements of the process as performed by others.
product liability	Legal responsibility of manufacturers, distributors and vendors of products to the end-user of the product, and to the public at large, to assure that the product is harmless when used for its intended purpose and in its intended manner.
professional corporation	Corporation formed for the purpose of conducting a profession such as medicine, law, accountancy, etc. Generally abbreviated as "PC" or "APC"
professional negligence	Malpractice. Failure of a professional to competently perform the functions of his or her profession in a manner consistent with the duty owed to the client or patient, and by reason of which the client or patient suffers loss, damage or harm. Breach of a professional duty.
proffer	To put something forward as an offering, as with proposed evidence, or a proposed payment.
profit	Financial gain. The difference between income and the total of costs and expenses.
profit and loss statement	See "income statement."
profit margin	The percentage of the selling price which is profit. (See also "margin" and "markup.")

prohibition	That which forbids certain acts or conduct.
promise	A firm commitment by a person (promisor) to perform an act, or to refrain from performing a particular act, or with respect to engaging or not engaging in particular conduct, upon which the person to whom the promise is given (promisee) may thereafter reasonably rely.
promissory estoppel	Court enforcement of a promise to avoid injustice when the person to whom the promise was made (promisee) acted in reliance on the promise, to his or her detriment, and the person making the promise (promisor) failed or refused to perform the promise.
promissory note	Written document which memorializes a loan, in which the borrower promises to repay the lender, setting forth the circumstances and terms of the loan and its intended repayment.
promo	That which is offered for purposes of product promotion. A specially-manufactured , non-royalty-earning copy of an album which is usually marked "For Promotional Use Only" and/or "Not for Sale." Absent a contract to the contrary, such albums require payment of mechanical royalties for the compositions included on them.
promoter	Person who organizes and who seeks or provides financing for a prospective business or event.
promotion	Campaign of advertising to excite interest in a particular product, enterprise, person, or event, often by the giving of benefits (premiums) to those who respond to the campaign.
proof	That which confirms or tends to confirm the truth of an alleged fact.

proof of service	Document which attests, under oath or under penalty of perjury, that a particular, identified document (process) has been served upon a party or parties, setting forth the date and manner of service, the persons upon whom served, and bearing the signature of the person who made the service (*e.g.*, process server.) Generally, the person making service may be anyone of legal age who is <u>not</u> a party to the action to which the served document relates.
property	Anything which is or can be owned.
property damage	Harm to real or personal property through another's intentional or negligent act or conduct.
propria persona	Literally, "one's proper person." *(Latin)* Oneself. In one's own name. (See, "*pro per.*")
proprietary	Referring to ownership or to a right of ownership.
proprietary interest	A right of ownership of property, either in whole or in part.
proprietary rights	Rights which are inherent to ownership. (*E.g.*, to use, occupy, control, etc.)
proprietor	Literally, an owner of any property, but particularly used in reference to the owner of a business.
proprietorship	Unincorporated business entity owned by a single person.
prosecute	To advocate for the plaintiff's case in a civil action, or the for government's case in a criminal case.
prosecutor	Attorney who appears for the government in a criminal case.

prospectus	Detailed document, governed by federal law, which is published by or on behalf of a business entity outlining the particular details of an issue of shares, debentures or other securities being offered for sale, and inviting the public to subscribe (invest) in the issue.
prove	To offer evidence and/or logical argument which demonstrates or tends to demonstrate that a particular proposition or allegation of fact is true.
provision	Separate and specific language appearing in a contract or other document, specifying certain conditions of agreement or anticipating future conditions, eventualities or requirements. Generally, the words "provision" and "clause" may be used interchangeably in referring to contract language, although technically a "clause" is a general term of a contract, whereas a "provision," relates to a potential occurrence. (See also, "clause.")
provisional remedy	General term for a court order which is intentionally temporary in effect, and which serves to protect persons or property pending some more permanent resolution of an issue. (See, *e.g.*, "preliminary injunction.")
proviso	A provision, as in a contract or agreement.
proximate	Immediate. Directly on or adjacent to. The closest point to another.
proximate cause	That which directly results in some specific new circumstance, condition, or event. Particularly, the action or conduct which directly results in an injury, loss, or harm.
proxy	Contraction of "procuracy," refers to the delegation of another to act in regard to some particular matter, particularly in regard to attending meetings and voting at such meetings. Also refers to the person to whom the delegation of authority is given. Thus one gives one's proxy (authorization) to one's proxy (person authorized to act.)

proxy fight	In corporate shareholder matters, where there are two or more groups having divergent views about a particular course of action, the battle between those groups to secure the larger number of proxies (votes) so as to control the outcome at an upcoming shareholders' meeting.
PRS	Acronym for "Performing Rights Society," a not-for-profit performing rights organization which grants licenses and collects royalties for composers, authors, songwriters and music publishers in the U.K. See "MCPS" and "MCPS-PRS Alliance."
prudent man rule	A rule governing investments made on behalf of another, not equally applied in all states. The rule provides that a fiduciary may only invest another's money only in such securities as would be purchased by a hypothetical prudent man of discretion and intelligence seeking a reasonable investment income and preservation of capital. In some states, the rule is superseded by an approved list of possible investments (the "legal list"), and certain fiduciaries (*e.g.,* pension fund trustees) are prohibited from purchasing any investment not on that list.
prudent man clause	In management agreements, particularly where the manager is given power of attorney or other authority to make investments or discretionary expenditures using the principal's funds, a clause which limits the nature of such expenditures or investments by some form of the "prudent man rule" requiring that no expenditures be made for unconventional or imprudent purposes.
pseudonym	Literally, a "false name." Fictitious name used in lieu of one's legal name. See "aka" and "pka."
pseudonymous	That which is done under a fictitious name.
public	(1) Referring to the nation, state, or entire community. (2) Open to all. (3) The people at large. The populace.

public benefit corporation	Term applied in some states to a not-for-profit (nonprofit) community-service corporation.
public charge	See "indigent."
public corporation	(1) Corporation formed to perform a governmental function, such as a city or town (municipal corporation) or other corporation formed in the public interest, supported in whole or part by public funds, and governed by managers deriving their authority from governmental appointment (*e.g.,* The National Endowment for the Arts.) (2) Often mistakenly used as a shortened form of "publicly-held corporation," referring to a privately owned company whose shares are publicly traded.
public defender	A government attorney, usually employed by a county for state matters, who provides legal services to criminal defendants, without fee, or on the basis of a reduced of deferred fee, based upon the defendant's limited ability or inability to pay for private counsel. (See also, "*in forma pauperis.*")
public domain	That which is freely available for use by the public, at large. In copyright law, the right of anyone to use literature, music, art or other creative works, without payment of royalty, after the period of copyright protection has expired, or when the work was created as a pubic work (*i.e,* government publications), or in instances where the copyright-owner has voluntarily placed the work into public domain.
public figure	Someone publicly known for who he or she is or has done. Those who have achieved positions of special prominence in society. Generally, anyone who has voluntarily or through circumstances become prominent in the public view, and thereby sacrificed significant portions of his or her right of privacy. In defamation (*i.e.,* slander and libel) actions, a more liberal, permissive standard is applied with respect to otherwise-defamatory statements made about public figures. (See "zone of privacy.")

public nuisance	A nuisance which affects, offends, or endangers some or all members of the public. Unreasonable interference with a right which is common to the public at large. (See "nuisance.")
public performance	One of the rights protected by copyright, the display, transmission, performance or recitation of a work, either in person or by mechanical or electronic means, presented to persons outside the scope of the copyright owner's family or associates.
public policy	General principle of law stating that no person may do anything which would tend to cause harm to the general public welfare. Certain types of acts are said to be "contrary to public policy," and while such acts are not illegal, *per se*, the law will refuse to confer benefits arising from such acts. Thus a contract which has the effect of violating public policy will not be enforced.
public property	Real or personal property owned by the government or by a government agency, although not necessarily available or accessible to the general public. (*E.g.*, nuclear warheads are public property.)
public record	Commonly, "public record" is taken to mean those documents which are generally available to all members of the public. (*E.g.*, deeds recorded on property title.) More properly, public records are any documents,. files, accounts, information, minutes, or other records which are maintained by the government or by a government agency, and which are maintained in the course of governmental activity. As with "public property," not all public records are available or accessible to the general public.
	Public records may, when properly authenticated or certified, be introduced into evidence. (See, "judicial notice." See also, "Freedom of Information Act.")
publication	(1) Act of making anything public by print, broadcast, or other means of general dissemination such that it is readily available to any portion of the public.
	(2) The tangible form in which an act of publication is manifested.

publish	To make public to at least one other person by any means.
Published Dealer Price	Wholesale price. Term often used in foreign markets instead of "wholesale." Generally abbreviated "PPD." The terms "Published Price to Dealer," "Net Price to Dealer" or "Base Price to Dealers" ("BPD") are sometimes used interchangeably.
Published Price to Dealers	Wholesale price. Term often used in foreign markets instead of "wholesale." Generally abbreviated "PPD." Alternatively, the terms "Published Dealer Price," "Net Price to Dealer" or "Base Price to Dealers" ("BPD") are sometimes used interchangeably.
puffing	Exaggeration of the good points of a product or service. Hype.
punish	To inflict harm upon another. (See "penalty.")
punishable	That which deserves punishment as a matter of law.
punishment	Any fine, confinement or penalty, up to and including the infliction of death, inflicted upon a person by operation of law and the sentence of a court. (See "penalty.")
punitive	Relating to punishment.
punitive damages	Damages awarded by a court in a civil action to punish a defendant for wrongful conduct, generally only awarded after proof that the conduct complained of was wanton, willful, malicious, oppressive, outrageous, and/or shocking to the conscience. Punitive damages are effectively identical to "exemplary" damages, differing only in the rationale underlying their imposition. (See "exemplary damages.")
purchase	(1) To obtain by payment of consideration. To buy. (2) A thing obtained for consideration. (3) The action of buying.

purchase order Request from a buyer to a vendor, usually written and with a numeric identification (*i.e.,* purchase order number), to provide specified goods or services upon stated terms. Common means of acceptance of an offer to sell. Generally abbreviated "PO."

putative Alleged; claimed; asserted as true; commonly believed or supposed to be true.

Q

q.v.	Abbreviation of *quod vide (Latin)*, meaning "which see." or colloquially "look at."
qua	As. In the capacity or nature of. *E.g.*, "Trustee *qua* trustee," refers to the trusteeship itself, as distinct from the person who holds that position.
quantum meruit	Literally, "as much as (he) deserved." Legal doctrine which provides that, in the absence of a valid contract, the party providing goods or services may still recover from the person receiving those goods or services, based solely on the fair value thereof. The doctrine seeks to avoid an unjust enrichment of one party, at the expense of another, from a technical defect or inadvertent error in forming a contract, or from failure of the parties to have formalized a contract. (See "quasi contract.")
quash	To set aside, annul or make void. A motion to quash seeks to have some prior act or process deemed void and of no effect. (*E.g.,* a motion to quash service of summons asks the court to find that there was no good service on a party, and therefore no jurisdiction for any subsequent action taken against that party in reliance on such jurisdiction.)
quasi	Literally, "as if." *(Latin)* Almost; similar to; analogous to; resembling.
quasi contract	Circumstance in which the court will, in the absence of a valid contract, nonetheless treat the parties as contracting parties, to avoid unjust enrichment of one party at the expense of the other.
quasi corporation	Business which has operated in all respects as though it were a corporation, without having yet completed the necessary formalities for incorporation.

quasi-criminal	Certain actions which the court may punish by fine or incarceration. (*E.g.,* contempt of court by violation of a civil court order.) Unless the offense occurred within the plain view and presence of the court (*i.e.,* direct contempt), a special proceeding is generally required, at which the party accused is afforded an opportunity to appear, defend, confront accusers, *etc.,* as in a criminal matter.
query	An inquiry; a question; an interrogatory. To pose a question to another.
question of fact	Those issues which are in dispute regarding specific occurrences, conduct and actions of parties, without respect to how those facts are to be interpreted. "What actually happened?," as distinct from "What is the legal effect of what happened?"
question of law	An issue which requires the application or interpretation of a point of law. The legal effect of proven facts, as distinct from the facts themselves.
quid pro quo	Literally, "(this) something for (that) something." *(Latin)* Mutual exchange of consideration between parties. Value to be given, in exchange for value received.
quiet enjoyment	Right to enjoy and use premises, without annoyance, hindrance, or encroachment.
quiet title	(1) Cause of action to establish true title to real or personal property, and to thereby silence all rival claimants. (1) To judicially determine the lawful ownership of property, nullifying all non-proven claims against it.
quit	To leave; depart; vacate. To abandon occupancy or claim of right.

quitclaim   Type of deed given without warranty of title, in which the person giving it conveys to another any and all such rights as he or she *may* have in respect to described real or personal property, without guarantee that any such right actually exists. *Cf.* "grant deed."

quorum   That number of members of a governing body who are required to be present before a meeting of that body can be lawfully conducted.

quotient verdict   Prohibited method of calculating an award of monetary damages, where each jury member writes the amount which that juror believes should be awarded, and the mathematical average (or other pre-agreed formula) determines the final amount. Verdicts based on chance or averaging are generally unlawful, and provide grounds for having the verdict or award set aside.

R

®	Symbol for "registered trademark" or "registered service mark," the "circle-R" symbol may only be used if official registration has, in fact, been obtained. (Prior to official registration, the "™" or "SM" symbols may be used.)
race rule	Common term for doctrine which provides that an earlier recorded document takes precedence over a later-recorded conflicting document.
Racketeer Influenced Corrupt Organizations Act (RICO)	Federal statutes (18 U.S.C. §§ 1961-1968) which provide for both criminal and/or civil prosecution of persons or entities engaged in certain types of criminal activities, characterized by a common enterprise, scheme and pattern of unlawful conduct.
racketeering	Federal crime of conspiring to form an organization and/or operating as an organization, the purpose of which organization includes the commission of crimes.
ransom	Money demanded by, or paid to, one who illegally takes and holds the person or property of another, in consideration for a promise that such person or property will be released upon delivery thereof. Generally, the money demanded by and/or paid to a kidnapper.
ratable	Proportional. Comparability of two or more values which are unequal. A quality of any two or more things which can be mathematically compared to each other.
ratification	Subsequent approval of, or acquiescence to, an action which was not previously approved by the person ratifying.

ratify	To confirm, adopt, or acquiesce in the act of another, after the fact, even though it may have been unknown or not approved in advance.
ready, willing and able	Having all of the necessary authority, intention, and means to perform.
real estate	Real property. Land, including all improvements and appurtenances constructed or growing thereon.
real party in interest	Person or entity materially affected, either beneficially or adversely, by the outcome of an action.
real property	Land, including all structures which are firmly attached thereto, all improvements permanently affixed to such structures, and all vegetation growing upon that land.
realty	A shortened form of the term, "real property."
reasonable	Just, rational, appropriate, ordinary or prudent. This is one of those apparently simple words which can lead to unforeseen consequences. What is "reasonable" to one party is often unreasonable to another, and use of the word in contracts and statutes leaves room for subsequent, discretionary interpretation.
reasonable care	Degree of caution and concern for the safety of oneself and of others that a normal, prudent and conscientious person would normally be expected to use.
reasonable doubt	Uncertainty. A perception that reasonable, alternative possibilities exist.
reasonable reliance	That level of trust which a prudent person would give to facts believed to be true in determining a course of action based on those supposed facts.
reasonable time	Amount of time usually and customarily required, within an industry, trade or profession, to perform some particular act or obligation.

rebate	Discount or deduction on sales price, usually paid separately to the purchaser at or after the time of purchase.
rebuttable presumption	A fact which the court is legally required to accept as true until sufficient evidence has been introduced to demonstrate to the contrary. (See "presumption")
rebuttal	Evidence or argument offered to contradict, counter, or disprove the argument or evidence introduced by an adverse party.
receipt	Written acknowledgment, signed by the recipient, affirming that a payment, or delivery of some other consideration, or of an object, has been received.
receiver	An impartial third-party, appointed by the court to take control of a property in dispute, pending adjudication of the respective rights of the disputing parties.
receivership	Manner of operation of a business or property under the control of a receiver. Such property or business is said to be "in receivership"
recess	Temporary break in a trial or other court proceedings, in a legislative session, or in a formal meeting.
recipient	One who receives something from another.
reciprocity	Mutual exchange of privileges, rights, or courtesies between states, nations, businesses, or other entities.
recital	A statement of facts. In contracts, the recitals generally state the facts underlying the contract and its general intention. Frequently, each separate recital commences with the word, "whereas," followed by a statement. In consequence, recitals are sometimes colloquially referred to as the "whereases."

reckless	Careless to the point of disregarding danger or possibility of harm to others, even though no harm was intended.
	Recklessness (disregarding danger) is more culpable conduct than negligence (unawareness of danger that a reasonable person would have perceived.)
reckless disregard	Voluntary gross negligence (breach of duty), either by commission or omission, without apparent concern for potential danger or harm to others.
reconsideration	Motion asking court to reconsider and modify its own prior ruling on an issue in light of newly discovered relevant facts or a change of relevant law, which was unknown or not available to the moving party at the time the matter was originally briefed and argued, or when the court initially ruled.
reconveyance	The cancellation of a deed of trust by the lender, upon satisfaction of debt, transferring title back to the property owner, free of that previously-recorded debt.
record (1)	(1) To transfer sounds onto a device capable of subsequently reproducing those sounds. To make a recording of speech, music, or other sounds, onto magnetic, electronic, or other, medium.
	(2) An object containing data which can be reproduced as audible sounds. (See, "phonorecord.")
	(3) A tangible object (*e.g.*, a writing) which memorializes certain transactions, facts or events.
record (2)	To deliver a document to the County Recorder of any county for the purpose of having the document made a matter of public record.
record club	Method of direct-marketing of recordings to consumers, usually at discounted prices. Under recording contracts, sales to record clubs generally earn reduced (or no) royalties for the Artist.

recording fund   In recording contracts, that portion of an advance which is designated as the budget for recording expenses. The artist, producer or other person receiving the advance is generally entitled to retain any portion of the recording fund not expended in the course of the recording process.

recordation   Act of filing a document as a public record.

records   All documentary material maintained by any person, business, governmental, or other entity, providing history and material details of correspondence, meetings, agreements, disputes, and transactions of every kind. In this context, "documentary" includes any method of preservation of data, including electronic and magnetic media.

recoup   To recover money previously expended.

recoupment   Right to recover sums previously expended by deduction from sums otherwise due to another. In the music industry, recoupment may be on an album-by-album basis or on a contract basis. In the latter, expenses (*e.g.,* advances) incurred in regard to one album may be recouped later from sales of a subsequent album.

recourse   Right of the holder of a negotiable instrument (*e.g.,* check) to seek payment from the maker or from any intervening endorser, unless the endorsement was made "without recourse."

recover   To obtain a sum to offset, in whole (recovery in full) or in part (partial recovery), a prior loss or expense.

recoverable   That portion of a loss or expense which can be recovered. (See "recoupment")

recovery   The sum of money, and the value of any other right or property received as a judgment, award or settlement of a claim of loss or expense.

recusal	Act of a judge, attorney, or other official in removing himself or herself from proceedings, usually on the grounds of conflict of interest, or possible bias in favor of, or against, one party or another in a dispute.
red herring	An apparently-important issue raised solely for the purpose of misdirecting attention away from true issues. The expression supposedly derives from a practice of dragging a smoked (and consequently red) herring across a trail to distract and misdirect pursuing dogs into following its pungent smell.
redline	Annotated draft document, showing deletions, additions and changes. Typically, deletions are indicated by a single, red horizontal line drawn through them, with additions shown in boldfaced or other distinguishing type.
redact	Act of editing a document copy by removal (or "blacking out") of portions thereof, usually to preserve confidentiality, secrecy, or privacy. The edited copy is thereafter referred to as a "redacted document."
redeem	To buy back that which one has previously conveyed or pledged. (*E.g.*, a mortgagor who pays the lender (mortgagee) in full thereby redeems the mortgage.) To perform a pledge or promise.
redress	1. To set right, remedy or rectify. 2. To make amends for. 3. Satisfaction for wrong done; reparation or correction. The right to petition the government for redress of grievances is guaranteed by the first amendment of the U. S Constitution.
referee	Impartial person to whom a dispute, or portion of a dispute, may be referred for consideration and recommendation as to how best to proceed. Upon consideration by a court, a referee's recommendations may be rejected, or adopted and converted into a court order, with or without modification by the court.

referendum Process whereby an existing law may be re-examined by voters, and either repealed or affirmed. Generally, the process of reexamining any regulation by putting it to a vote.

reformation Correction or change of an existing document by court order.

regulations Rules and administrative codes issued by governmental agencies.

rehearing To conduct a hearing upon an issue previously heard, upon the granting of a party's motion for such rehearing, or on the order of a higher court, or *sua sponte*. Generally, a rehearing occurs when there has been a mistake of fact or law in the conduct of a prior hearing, or when new relevant facts which could not reasonably have been known are discovered after the prior hearing, or when relevant law has changed since the prior hearing. See also, "reconsideration."

reimburse To repay a previously-expended sum to the person who expended it.

reimbursable An expenditure for which one may obtain repayment. A "reimbursable" advance requires the artist to repay it in event that it is not recouped through sales.

reimbursement Repayment of a previously expended sum.

release	(1) To give up a right by releasing another from an obligation to the person giving the release. Also, the written instrument by which such release is given. A release may be a "partial release," releasing only part of a claim (see also, "pro tanto,"), or a "general release," giving up all known claims. Also, by the inclusion of highly specific language, a general release may eliminate other legitimate claims which the person giving the release (releasor) does not know exist. Caution should be therefore be exercised in signing any release. (See "known and unknown")
	(2) Permission to use another's name, voice, likeness or biographical material in connection with a commercial venture. (See "door release.")
relegate	To transfer or assign to an inferior position, division or rank.
relevancy	The degree to which proffered evidence has some material and reasonable connection with or in regard to a particular matter which is at-issue or under consideration.
relevant	Having some reasonable connection with or in regard to the particular matter which is at-issue or under consideration.
reliance	Acting upon the supposed truth of another's statement, or representation, or person's purported good reputation.
relief	General term for any benefit which can be conferred by court order.
remainder	That which is left after distribution.
remand	To send back. On appeal, unless judgment is affirmed, the appellate court will remand (send a case back) to the trial court, with instructions to either modify its judgment consistent with the appellate opinion, or to retry all or a portion the case as directed by the opinion.

remedy	General term for the means which a party may employ to seek satisfaction of a claim or enforcement of a right.
remittitur	(1) Final document issued by a court of appeal, returning the record and proceedings to the lower court. (2) Procedure by which the monetary amount a jury verdict is reduced by the court.
remote	Distant in location or time; far off; of only slight possibility.
removal	Transfer of a case from one court to another, on jurisdictional or other grounds. Usually, removal implies the transfer of a state court case to federal court.
renewal	Agreement to continue an existing arrangement for an additional period of time. The right of renewal may be contained within a contract, so that it vests in one party or another, who may renew at their sole option.
rent	(1) To obtain the use of real or personal property from another for a period of time, for a fee. (2) The fee paid for use of the property of another.
renunciation	An affirmative statement by which one permanently gives up a present or future right or benefit.
reorganization	Implementation of a plan to restructure a business. Reorganization under the auspices of the U.S. Bankruptcy Code is commonly referred to as Chapter 11. A modified version of such bankruptcy reorganization is also available to small businesses and to individuals under Chapter 13 of the Bankruptcy Code. (See "Chapter 11" and "Chapter 13.")
repair	To restore to functionality.
repeal	The annulment of an existing law by passage of a new law which declares the former law to be no longer effective as of a certain past, present or future date.

replevin	Common law action to regain possession of one's personal property (chattels) from another who holds that property wrongfully. (See "attachment.")
reports	The published decisions of appeals courts.
repossess	To take back one's property by lawful means.
representation	(1) A statement of purported material fact. (2) One's agency or manager. (3) One's legal counsel.
representative	(1) An agent. One who is empowered to speak for another. (2) Condition of being essentially identical to a larger number of like things, such that inspection of the one is sufficient surety as to the nature and condition of the remainder. *I.e.,* a "representative sample."
repudiation	Denial of the existence of a contract or the binding effect of a portion of a contract. A refusal to perform based on a claim that one is not obligated to do so. (See also, "anticipatory breach.")
repugnant	That which the law and society finds abhorrent, wholly unacceptable, and vile.
reputation	Community opinion of a person or entity. One's good name and character.
reputed	That which is generally held to be true, as a matter of reputation, without proof.
request	To ask or demand of someone that they do or refrain from doing something.
res	Literally, "thing." *(Latin)* The subject matter or object of any communication, discussion, or dispute.

res gestae	Literally, "things done," *(Latin)*, provides an exception to the hearsay rule, admitting testimony as to conduct and speech of another proximate to the occurrence which is at-issue. (See "excited utterance.") In its broader sense, *res gestae* embraces the whole of an occurrence or transaction under consideration, and every part of it.
res ipsa loquitur	Literally, "the thing speaks for itself." *(Latin)* Rebuttable presumption of liability arising upon showing of injury from an event which would not normally occur without negligence. The burden then shifts to the defendant to disprove his or her wrongful conduct. In actions where the *res ipsa loquitur* doctrine applies, plaintiff need only show injury and fact that injury was caused by that which was under defendant's control.
res judicata	Literally, "the thing has been judged." *(Latin)* Alternatively, "*res adjudicata.*" Rule which prohibits any court from making a ruling or judgment upon any particular issue or case which has previously been judged upon on its merits by another court which had jurisdiction over the issue and the parties or their privies. (See "privity.") (See also, "collateral estoppel.")
resale	To sell to another that which includes, in whole or in part, that which one has acquired through purchase. (*E.g.*, The retail sale of items purchased wholesale, in grater numbers. Also, the sale of a manufactured item which includes purchased components.)
resale license	Exemption from payment of sales tax on items which are not purchased for use or consumption, but rather for sale to others, or for inclusion as part of a product to be sold to others.
rescind	To withdraw from a contract, restoring the parties to the position which each had prior to such contract.

rescission   Cancellation of a contract by mutual agreement of the parties, or by court judgment on a cause of action for rescission, based upon an alleged legal defect in the formation of that contract.

reservation   Provision in contract or deed which retains (reserves) for one party some right or benefit which otherwise would be considered a part of consideration being exclusively conveyed to the other party.

reserve fund   Fund provided by terms of contract for the purpose of withholding monies to be later utilized for certain specified, foreseeable types of costs or expenses relating to the subject matter of the contract. In recording contract, a reserve fund is generally a fixed percentage of earned royalties held back as a setoff for future returns or other royalty adjustments.

reserves   See "reserve fund."

residence   Place where a natural person maintains his or her home, or where a business was initially incorporated, or where it maintains its principal offices. Residence may be critical to a determination of proper jurisdiction.

resident   Person who lives in a particular place as his or her primary place of residence. A business is deemed a resident of the state where it was formed and under the laws of which it operates, or of the state in which it maintains its principal place of business.

residue   That which is left following distribution. The remainder.

resisting arrest   Crime of using any amount of physical force to hamper, impede or delay one's lawful arrest by a police officer.

resolution   Statement of policy made by a governing body (*e.g.,* a corporation's board of directors), generally specifying the reasons for such policy, the policy itself, and authorizing actions to be taken by designated persons to implement such policy.

respondeat superior	Literally, "let the master answer." *(Latin)* Legal doctrine which provides that the master (employer) is legally liable for the acts or omissions of the servant (employee) done in the normal course and scope of that employment.
respondent	Party required to answer a petition for relief. (*I.e.,* the defendant in certain types of actions.) Also, in appellate practice, the party against whom the appeal is filed. The respondent in an appellate writ proceeding may be a lower court, and any response will be filed not by the respondent but by a "real party in interest." (*i.e.,* by the adverse party in the underlying case.)
responsible	(1) Having the capacity and ability to make competent decisions and to accept the consequences thereof. (2) Being legally liable or accountable.
Restatement	The Restatements are scholarly works of fundamental legal precepts common to most jurisdictions throughout the United States, prepared by the American Law Institute. They are differentiated by the area of law which each addresses, as well as by their edition numbers. (*E.g.,* Second Restatement of Torts, *etc.*) The Restatements are frequently cited as authority in legal pleadings.
restitution	The restoration of property (or an equivalent monetary sum) to the proper owner of such property.
restraining order	A temporary form of injunctive relief, issued by a court and effective for a very short time, usually only until the matter may be given a full hearing, at which time the order may be extended, dissolved, modified, or replaced by a more formal injunction.
restraint of trade	Any unilateral or collusive activity which unlawfully restricts or interferes with another's manufacture, marketing, or sale of goods or services.
restriction	A limitation on activity imposed by contract, court order, statute, regulation or ordinance.

result	An outcome. Final determination of an issue or case. Ultimate recovery.
resulting trust	Involuntary trust implied by law and imposed by court order, based upon circumstances which present *indicia* of a trust, even though no trust was intended by either the trustor or the trustee. (See "constructive trust.")
retainer	Advance payment to a professional (*e.g.*, attorney) to secure his or her employment in regard to services to be performed.
retract	To formally withdraw (take back) a prior written or spoken statement.
retraction	A formal withdrawal of a prior written or spoken statement.
retrial	New trial granted upon the motion of the losing party, or by the order of a higher court on appeal.
retroactive	That which has effect from a date earlier than its enactment. That which is effective backward in time.
return allowance	Provision in recording contracts permitting record label to withhold a stated percentage of earned royalties to allow for possible returns of previously distributed copies not sold at retail. (See "reserve fund.")
return privilege	Privilege afforded to distributors to return unsold merchandise, usually for trade credit against future orders.
returns	Albums previously sold to distributors, but subsequently returned by distributor to label under a "return privilege" agreement. Under the terms of most recording agreements, returns are excluded from royalty calculations. (See "actually sold," and "reserve fund.")
reuse	The use of a prior recording in a different medium, as when a recorded master from an album is later used in a film soundtrack.

reuse fee	Fee payable to performers on a recording when that recording is subsequently used in a different medium. (See "reuse.")
reversal	Decision which vacates a prior court ruling and replaces it with an opposite ruling. A court may reverse itself, or reversal may be ordered by a higher court, on appeal.
reversible error	Legal mistake made or permitted by the trial court which is so significant that it merits reversal of the trial court's ruling or judgment.
reversion	Return to the original owner (or successors) of rights, benefits or property previously conveyed.
revert	To return to a previous or original relationship, situation or position.
review	Appellate consideration of a lower court's judgment. Review of appellate court decisions may be granted by a state's court of last resort (*E.g.,* state's highest court.)
revocation	Cancellation or annulment of a contract either by the mutual consent of the parties or by court judgment upon a cause of action for revocation.
revoke	To cancel or annul a previous act, such as a statement, contract, instrument, or authorization.
RIAA	Acronym for "Recording Industry Association of America," which is the primary trade association for the U.S. recording industry. Based in Los Angeles, the RIAA collects and tabulates music sales and trend data, awards Gold, Platinum and (most recently) Diamond Albums for U.S. sales, and is at the forefront of efforts to combat music piracy.
RICO	See "Racketeer Influenced Corrupt Organizations Act"
rider	Attachment to a document which adds to, modifies, or amends the document to which it is attached. (See "addendum.")

right	That to which one is entitled, either by law or by lawful contract. An entitlement which flows from so-called "natural law."
right of first refusal	See "first refusal."
right to audit	See "auditing provision."
riot	A violent disturbance of peace by an indeterminable number of persons.
ripe	Referring to issues which are fully developed, such that a court may properly adjudicate them. A case which presents issues of societal significance which the Supreme Court wishes to address.
risk	That which contains a danger of loss, damage or harm.
roadie	Stagehand employed by a band, performer or promoter to travel with the show.
robbery	The taking of property directly from the person of another.
royalty	Fee due to the owner of a licensable right (*e.g.,* copyright; patent) from the licensee for use of such right.
royalty base	That sum upon which royalty calculations will be based. It is generally tied to SRLP or PPD.
royalty provision	That portion of a recording contract which specifies the rate, basis (see "royalty base"), manner and frequency of royalty payments. The rate may be expressed as fixed sum per unit, or (more usually) as a percentage of sales. It may also specify limitations such as restricting royalties to units "actually sold" through "normal retail channels," and may exclude or limit royalties for "free goods" and discounted sales.

rpm	Revolutions per minute. Analogue phonograph records are commonly identified by the rotational speed at which they are to be replayed. The common speeds are 45-rpm (singles), 78-rpm (older singles), and 33⅓-rpm (albums). See "vinyl."
rule	(1) A regulation, requirement, or restriction. (2) To authoritatively decide a legal question.
rules of court	Body of procedural regulations adopted by courts for their own governance. Although rules have the force of (procedural) law, they are of lesser authority than statutes, which are enacted by the legislature.
ruling	Court decision regarding a legal question, a case, or an issue presented within a case.
running with the land	Rights, benefits, covenants, restrictions, easements, and other matters recordable against title to real property, and which remain attached to that property regardless of a change of the property's ownership.

S

§	Standard typographical symbol for "section," it is pluralized by doubling; *i.e.*, "§§," for "sections."
ss.	Abbreviation for a statement of venue, generally found adjacent to a recital of the location (nation, state, county) where an instrument has been executed.
/ss/	Conventional mark used at signature line of document copy, indicating that the original of that document has been signed, and usually followed by the printed name of the signatory.
SAG	Acronym for "Screen Actors' Guild," a craft union which represents film and television actors in the United States.
salient	Prominent; important. Particularly noteworthy, relevant and material. The "high points" of an issue or agreement.
sampling	Use of a portion of a prior recording within a newly-recorded work.
sanction	Penalty imposed by court upon a party or attorney, generally for a procedural offense, bad faith tactic, or a contempt. Sanctions can be monetary or substantive, including evidence preclusion, issue preclusion, or dismissal of cause of action or suit.
sane	Of normal mental condition. One who knows the difference between right and wrong anc appreciates the consequences of his or her actions. (See, "insanity.")
satisfaction	Receiving that to which one is entitled, in whole or in part.

satisfaction of judgment	Document signed by judgment creditor affirming that the judgment debtor has paid all or part of an outstanding judgment debt. If paid in full, it is referred to as a "Full Satisfaction of Judgment," and if only paid in part, it is referred to as a "Partial Satisfaction of Judgment." (See, "*pro tanto.*")
satisfactory	That which is sufficient to the purpose for which it is intended. (But see, "technically satisfactory.")
save harmless	See "hold harmless" and "indemnify."
scale	Minimum amount payable to union members for their performance. Scale varies based upon the particular union (*e.g.,* AFTRA, AFM) and on the services performed.
scienter	Literally, "having knowledge." *(Latin)* In certain legal matters, and particularly in criminal matters, a party's actual knowledge of some fact, circumstance or condition is material to a determination of their liability or culpability. (See also, "knew or should have known.")
scintilla	Literally, "spark." *(Latin)* Used in reference to a minuscule, barely-discernable amount. Frequently used in the negative, as in "not a scintilla," meaning none whatsoever.
scope of employment	The entire range of any actions or activities in which an employee may reasonably be engaged during performance of his work in furtherance of the employer's interests, and for the consequences of which his or her employer is therefore liable. (See, "*respondent superior.*")
screener	Copy of audiovisual work provided to industry members for their consideration in voting for upcoming awards.

scrivener	One who writes a document for another, usually for a fee, but who contributes no creative element to the content of the document. A scribe.
SDT	Acronym for *"subpoena duces tecum"*
seal	(1) An object or device which creates an image or impression upon paper or melted wax, with discernable patterns, symbolic emblems, and/or words, for the purpose of authentication and/or to prevent undetected tampering. (2) To affix one's seal to a document. (3) To enclose a document or other object in such a manner as to prevent it being opened without detection.
sealed records	Judicial records which the court orders kept secret, and which are therefore not generally accessible. (See, *"in camera."*)
sealed verdict	Jury verdict which has not yet been publicly announced, and which the court may therefore ordered sealed until such announcement.
search	To look for something. To go onto, into and/or through another's property for the purpose of obtaining evidence. There are constitutional protections, as well as numerous laws and rules, which govern lawful searches, a violation of which may cause the search to be deemed improper and preclude evidence obtained from or by reason of such search. (See, "fruit of the poisonous tree," "plain view," and "search and seizure.")
search warrant	Written order by a judge, given in reliance upon a police officer's affidavit or declaration and such other evidence as may be presented, which permits law enforcement officers to enter a location which is particularly described in the warrant, and to search for and seize evidence which falls within the scope of items which are also particularly described within the warrant. (*Q.v.*, U.S. Constitution, 4th Amendment.)

secret rebate	See "kickback."
secretary	(1) A clerical and administrative office assistant. (2) The chief administrative officer of a corporation or other organization. (3) Head of a governmental department.
section	A division of a code; a statute. The word "section" is usually abbreviated by the typographical symbol, §, which is doubled (§§) (sections) when more than one section is cited.
secured transaction	Any agreement in which real or personal property is pledged as collateral (security) for an obligation, such that the property may become forfeit in the event of non-performance.
securities	General term for shares of stock, bonds, and debentures.
security deposit	Payment required by a lessor from a lessee to assure that rented property will be returned in good condition.
security interest	General term for a right in real or personal property, held by a lender or other person with an interest such property as being the collateral for an obligation.
sedition	Crime of advocating a violent overthrow of government.
seizure	Taking by law enforcement officers of potential evidence.
self-defense	Use of reasonable force against a person to protect oneself, others, or property, from harm being inflicted or which is about to be inflicted by that person.
self-executing	Those provisions of law or of a contract which are immediately effective, without requiring further action or legislation.

self-help	Obtaining relief or enforcing one's rights without resorting to judicial process or police assistance. Self-help is judicially disfavored, and may in some instances be cause for a civil or criminal complaint against the person utilizing such methods. (*E.g.,* A civil complaint for wrongful eviction, etc., and/or a charge of criminal trespass against a landlord who conducts a "self help" eviction of a tenant.)
self-incrimination	The making of a statement which implicates the person making it in some criminal act. No person may be compelled to thus incriminate himself or herself, and may therefore lawfully refuse to answer questions requiring such statements as a truthful. (*Q.v.,* U.S. Constitution, 5th Amendment.) No legal inference may be drawn from such refusal.
self-serving	Statement which has as its purpose a bolstering of the position of the person making it. A question asked of a party to a lawsuit which must necessarily lead to a response which has only such bolstering effect. Generally, such questions are objectionable as hearsay, unless they fall within one of the exceptions (*e.g.,* state of mind.)
sell	Transfer of possession and ownership of real or personal property, for consideration.
sentence	Judicial announcement of the punishment to be imposed upon a person convicted of a crime. The punishment imposed by a court upon criminal conviction.
separate property	In community property states (*e.g.,* Arizona, California, Texas, ...) property which is not communal, but which is owned separately by one spouse alone.
separation agreement	Agreement between two married people who have agreed to separate from each other, without filing for dissolution of their marriage.
sequester	To keep separate or apart.

seriatim	Literally, "in series," *(Latin)* refers to distinct acts or occurrences which are sequential; one following another.
servant	An employee. Anyone who works for another (the employer), in furtherance of the employer's purposes.
serve	To deliver legal documents by an approved method to a person or party for whom they are intended.
serve and file rule	As a general rule having but few exceptions (*e.g.,* proofs of service) each and every document filed with the court must be served upon all parties who have previously appeared in the action. Many jurisdictions will refuse to accept a document for filing unless a signed proof of service is attached.
service (1)	Work performed by another person, for consideration.
service (2)	The act of delivering legal documents to another person in a manner prescribed by law.
service by FAX	Delivery of legal documents by telefacsimile (FAX). Not permitted in all jurisdictions or in respect to certain types of legal documents, which may require a more formal service. (See "personal service")
service by mail	Delivery of legal pleadings by depositing them into the U.S. Mail, with fully-prepaid postage. Such documents are considered to have been served on the day they are mailed, but the receiving party is generally permitted a specified number of additional days in which to respond to them, to allow for delay between mailing and receipt. Service by mail is not permitted in respect to certain types of legal documents, which may require a more formal service.(See "personal service")

service by publication	In an instance where the person to be served cannot be located or served by other means, despite diligent attempts, the court may permit service to be deemed completed upon the publication of the document in a "newspaper of general circulation" in one or more counties. The court order for such publication will specify the number of days during which such publication must occur, and service is deemed complete upon presenting the court with proof that such publication has been completed. Publication is often a costly process, but may be the only means of obtaining lawful jurisdiction over a party who successfully avoids personal service.
service of process	Delivery of copies of legal pleadings, including summons, complaint, petition, motions, hearing notices, orders, discovery, *etc.*, by a means of delivery prescribed by law.
services	Work performed by others, for consideration.
SESAC	Originally incorporated under the name "Society of European Stage Authors and Composers," SESAC is a privately-owned performing rights organization, headquartered in Nashville, with offices in New York, Los Angeles, and London.
set	To schedule; to fix a date upon, or before, or after which something is to occur or commence.
set aside	To negate, annul or make void.
setoff	See "offset."
setting	The act of scheduling a date.
settle	To resolve a dispute through negotiation and compromise, before a final court judgment is announced.

settled statement	A written statement of what has previously occurred in the course of litigation, used in cases where there is no official court reporter's transcript of those proceedings. (See also, "agreed statement.")
settlement	Resolution of a dispute prior to judgment, through negotiation and compromise. The document which embodies the terms and conditions of settlement.
settlement conference	Court proceeding, usually conducted by a judge or court officer other than the trial judge, in an effort to bring a dispute to resolution without trial.
settlor	Person who creates and initially funds a trust by declaration of trust, identifying the purpose, principal assets, trustee and beneficiaries of that trust. The trustor.
severability clause	Contract provision which states that, if any portion of the contract is found to be invalid, unlawful, or contrary to public policy, the remainder of the contract shall nonetheless continue in full force and effect, without the invalidated (severed) provision or, conversely, which agrees that the entire contract is to be voided if any portion is held invalid.
severable contract	Agreement made up of two or more separate contracts which are not necessarily dependent on each other. *E.g.,* a record company may have separate contracts with each artist in a group, each of which is severable from the others unless there are specific provisions to the contrary in each contract.
several liability	Responsibility of one party (obligor) to pay or perform an entire obligation, rather than merely a share of that obligation, regardless of the existence of co-obligors.
severance	The act of separating one thing from another, either voluntarily or by court order. Termination of employment, separating an employee from his employer and job.

sexual harassment — Unwanted sexual approaches, whether verbal, by conduct, or physical contact, directed at another by reason of his or her gender, resulting in emotional distress or other personal injury. Actionable as a tort, and most frequently occurring in workplace-related settings. An employer who engages in such conduct, or knowingly permits employees to engage in or continue such conduct, may be held liable for damages. (See *"respondent superior"* and "zero tolerance.")

shall — Must. An imperative, mandatory command; without option or choice. Distinguishing between the mandatory "shall," and the permissive "may," is critical in interpreting contracts, orders, and statutes.

share — (1) A portion of a benefit.
(2) A single unit of stock in a company.

share certificate — Document issued by a corporation, signed by designated officers and (usually) bearing the corporate seal, representing ownership of a stated number of shares of a stated type of stock in that corporation. The certificate may also bear certain restrictions relating to timing or the manner in which those shares may be traded or sold. Also referred to as a "stock certificate."

share and share alike — Phrase referring to division of a benefit into equal portions to be distributed equally among all beneficiaries. See *"pari passu."*

shareholder — An owner of one or more shares of stock in a corporation.

shareholders' agreement — Agreement among the shareholders of a small (closely held) corporation, providing for the corporation itself, or one or more of the other shareholders, to have the option to purchase the shares of a shareholder who dies, becomes disabled or is otherwise disqualified from maintaining an active role in the corporation's business.

shareholders' derivative action	Lawsuit filed by a corporate shareholder, in his or her own name, but where the corporation is the proper plaintiff, on the basis that the corporation itself is entitled to file such suit, and should have filed such suit, but has failed or refused to do so.
shareholders' meeting	Meeting, usually annual, of all (or a quorum) of shareholders of a corporation, primarily for the purpose of electing a board of directors. (See "proxy.")
shepardize	Method of legal research which cross-references cases and statutes to subsequent court opinions which cite and/or comment upon those statutes or earlier cases. Essential in determining whether or not a particular citation remains effective for its intended purpose, or has been distinguished, disapproved, superseded, or modified by later decisions.
sheriff	Law enforcement officer for a county, usually elected.
sheriff's sale	Auction sale of property held by the sheriff pursuant to a court order.
shield laws	Statutes which (in some jurisdictions) permit journalists to refuse to produce their work product (notes and research) or to identify their sources of information.
shopping agreement	Contract authorizing another, for a fixed term, to act as an agent for the purpose of soliciting potential purchasers of a composition or a recording contract for an artist or group. Shopping agreements may be exclusive or non-exclusive, although most agents will insist on at least a period of exclusivity during which to attempt to find a buyer or a recording deal.
shift of burden	That which results from plaintiff having met its burden of proof, whereupon it falls to the defendant to disprove liability.
short cause	Lawsuit which the attorneys estimate can be tried in a relatively short period of time.

shortening time	Court order, made upon a party's motion or *sua sponte*, reducing the statutory amount of time generally afforded to perform some act. Thus a motion which might normally require three week's notice before hearing could be heard sooner, with the dates for filing an opposition and a reply reduced accordingly. Such order is generally referred to as an "OST."
show cause order	See "order to show cause."
sic	Thus. So. *(Latin)* Used, usually in parentheses, to denote that what precedes it is quoted precisely from another source, even though obviously erroneous or misspelled. *E.g.*, "This can bee *(sic)* a useful word."
side	A recorded composition.
side letter	Written, binding promise by an individual to perform services which are the subject of a separate agreement to which that individual is not personally a party. (See, "all in" and "loan out.") The term "side letter" is also sometimes used in reference to a "commitment letter" or "inducement letter."
side man	A non-principal musician performing in or with a group.
sidebar	(1) The area immediately adjacent to the judge's bench. (2) An off-the-record conference between attorneys and the judge which takes place in that location.
sign	(1) A posted notice. (2) To write one's name on a document to indicate agreement or ratification.
signatory	(1) Person who signs a document. (2) Person authorized to sign on behalf of a corporation or other entity.

silent partner	Investor who puts money into a business but takes no part in the management or operations of that business. Unless the business has been formally organized as other than a general partnership, a "silent" partner may nonetheless be personally liable for the business' obligations. (*Cf.,* "limited partner.")
similarly situated	In common circumstances; alike as to situation. In class action suits, the plaintiff(s) appear in their own name and on behalf of an entire, unnamed class of others who are "similarly situated." to the plaintiff(s).
sine qua non	Literally, "without which, not." *(Latin)* That which is fundamental and essential. The basic reason and purpose, without which there is no reason to proceed.
single	A commercial release containing only one or two recordings.
single accounting unit	Term used in connection with cross-collateralization, indicating that all royalties from all sources – including (without limitation) author's royalties, producer's royalties and artist's royalties – are attachable for purposes of recoupment.
situs	"Location" *(Latin)* The place where an incident occurred.
slander	Defamation of another by spoken word. (See "defamation" and "libel.")
small claims	The most junior civil court in most states, operated on the city or county level and having strictly limited jurisdiction to hear and adjudicate suits for monetary damages up to a certain amount . (*E.g.,* $5.000.00)
small right	The right to perform a musical work publicly and for profit, either through live performance or by broadcast.

SOCAN	Society of Composers, Authors and Music Publishers of Canada. A performing rights organization headquartered in Toronto, with offices throughout Canada.
sole proprietorship	Business owned by a single person or household, which is personally liable for the business' obligations.
solicitation of crime	Crime of encouraging or inducing another to commit a criminal act.
solicitor	In the United Kingdom, an attorney who provides all legal services except making court appearances. (See, "barrister.")
Solicitor General	Chief trial attorney in the Department of Justice, it is the office which generally appears for the United States before the Supreme Court.
solvency	Having sufficient funds to pay debts. Having assets in excess of liabilities.
song	An artistic work which combines words (lyrics) and music (composition) as an integrated whole.
songwriter	Author of songs.
sounds in	Referring to the underlying, basic legal theory for a lawsuit or dispute. *E.g.*: Personal injury sounds in tort, whereas non-performance of obligation sounds in contract.
south of the versus	Defendant in a lawsuit. One whose name appears below the "*vs.*" on the title page of the complaint.
speaking motion	Motion made in open court, without prior notice or a written pleading.
spec	Colloquial abbreviation for "speculative" or "speculation."

special appearance	Representation by an attorney in court for a limited purpose only, without making a general appearance on behalf of a party and thereby submitting that party to the court's *in personam* jurisdiction over him or her.
special damages	Damages which may be prayed and/or awarded for out-of-pocket expenses incurred as a necessary consequence of the incident which it the subject of the suit, although not proximately cause by that incident. (*E.g.,* Costs incurred in reasonable, good faith, lawful attempts to recover converted (stolen) property, prior to filing suit.)
special master	Person, usually an attorney, appointed by the court to carry out a court order, usually requiring particular knowledge or discretion.
special payments fund	AFM fund consisting of mandatory contributions from signatory record companies, based on a percentage of records sold. More fully referred to as the "Sound Recording Manufacturers' Special Payments Fund" (SRMSPF)
special prosecutor	Attorney from outside government service, appointed for the purpose of independently investigating and/or prosecuting a government agency or official.
special verdict	Jury findings, usually in writing on a form approved by the court, as to its specific answers to individual questions of fact presented by the case. (*E.g.,* "1. Was there a contract? (Yes or No) [If 'No,' proceed to question #17.]")
specific performance	Cause of action by which a party may obtain judgment by a court order which compels another party to perform contract obligations.
speculative	(1) Based on conjecture or supposition rather than on actual knowledge or certainty. Risky. (2) Evidentiary objection where question calls for witness to respond by guessing (speculating) rather than by stating a fact actually known.

speculative damages	Possible financial loss or expenses claimed by a plaintiff which have no clear basis in fact, but are based solely on possibilities rather than evidence. Damages which are only speculative are not permitted, and will not be awarded.
speculation	High risk investment undertaken in expectation of disproportionately high return. See "venture capital."
speedy trial	Right of criminal defendant to demand that there be no unreasonable delay between arrest and trial.
split advance	An advance which is payable in two or more installments, usually based on occurrence of particular events, such as contract signing, commencement of recording sessions, delivery of satisfactory master recordings, etc.
spontaneous exclamation	Sudden statement caused by the speaker having seen a surprising occurrence or event. An exception to the hearsay rule. (See, "*res gestae*" and "excited utterance.")
spousal support	Voluntary, contractual, or court-ordered payment(s) made by one spouse (or ex-spouse) to and for the financial support and maintenance of the other.
SRLA	"Sound Recording Labor Agreement." The master agreement between record companies and the AFM..
SRLP	Acronym for "Suggested Retail List Price," the term is used extensively in recording contracts in the U.S. and Canada as the basis for calculating artist's royalties. See also, "PPD."
SRMSPF	"Sound Recording Manufacturers' Special Payments Fund" (See "Special Payments Fund.")
stakeholder	Person having possession, custody, and/or control (*i.e.,* holding) the money or property of another, in which the holder thereof asserts no interest. A stakeholder in one in position to interplead money or property of another into court. (See "escrow," and "interpleader.")

standard of care   That degree of attention, caution, conscientiousness, and prudence which an ordinary, reasonable person could be expected to exercise under circumstance similar to those presented by the matter under consideration.

standard of proof   The degree to which a burden of proof must be demonstrated in a particular case. There are tree basic standards of proof: In criminal matters, the prosecution's burden is to prove guilt "beyond a reasonable doubt, and to the point of moral certainty." In civil matters, the higher standard is "clear and convincing evidence," and the lower standard is "a preponderance of the evidence."

stand, the   Chair occupied by a witness testifying in court, usually located to the side of the judge's bench closest to the jury. When called to testify, a witness is said to "take the stand," and while testifying to be "on the stand."

standing   The right to file or defend a lawsuit regarding particular matters, as a real party having a direct interest and privity with respect to the facts, occurrences, issues, and outcome of such action. It is fundamental that one without standing in regard to the subject matter of an action has no right to appear as a party in such action.

stare decisis   Policy of courts to stand by establish precedent and not disturb previously-decided points of law. Doctrine by which the law reflects not only statutes, but the entire body of published judicial opinions which interpret and explain those statutes and their application to particular types of issue.

state   (1) Any sovereign nation, or the government thereof.

(2) Any one of the several states of the United States.

(3) The government of the United States or of any of the several states, including all of their various departments and agencies.

state of domicile	The state in which a person has his or her permanent residence, or the state under the laws of which a business entity was formed and is maintained.
state of residence	The state in which a person has his or her principal place of residence, or the state in which a business entity maintains its principal offices or business operations.
status conference	Pre-trial meeting of attorneys before a judge, to discuss the present status of the case (*e.g.,* discovery, etc.) and to set dates for future proceedings.
statute	Federal or state written law enacted by Congress or by a state legislature.
statute of frauds	Law which requires that certain types of agreements must be made in writing, and not orally. Most notably (and historically) an agreement affecting title to real property must be made in writing. Additionally, writings are generally required for a contract made in consideration of marriage, a contract for more than one year, an agreement by an executor to pay for estate expenses, a contract for goods valued at more than $500 (excepting professional and custom goods), and a promise to pay the debt of another.
statute of limitations	Law governing period of time allowed between actionable occurrence and last date upon which a complaint may be filed in respect to that occurrence. The period varies from state to state, and runs from as little as a matter of days to ten years or more, depending upon the underlying cause of action or criminal charge. In some criminal matters (*e.g.,* murder) there is no statute of limitations.
statutory	On the basis of a written law. See "*de jure*" and "*malum prohibitum.*"

statutory rate	The royalty rate fixed by law, payable to the copyright owner of a composition (publisher), unless there is an agreement (mechanical license) specifying a lower rate. (See, "compulsory license.") As of January 2006, the statutory rate per track was raised to 9.1¢ for five minutes or less, with an additional 1.75¢ for each minute or fraction over five minutes.
stay	A court-ordered or statutory moratorium on some or all further proceedings in an action.
stay away order	Court order commanding a person to stay some minimum distance from some other person or location. (See, "injunction" and "TRO.")
step out	Short, featured performance by one or more musicians or vocalists during performance in which they are otherwise non-featured. Under union contracts, step-out performances are entitled to additional, above-scale payment.
stet	Literally, "let it stand." *(Latin)* Notation made in the course of editing a draft document, indicating that a prior correction should be stricken, and the original text reinstated.
stipulation	Agreement between parties' counsel which is binding upon the parties, usually with respect to procedural or factual issues relating to an action. In some matters (*e.g.*, continuing a trial date), court approval and an order may be necessary, since attorneys cannot, by agreement, usurp the court's authority to control its own process and calendar.
stock	(1) Goods or products (inventory) on hand for sale by a business. (2) Shares in a corporation.
stock certificate	See "share certificate."
stock in trade	The product, goods, or services in which a business regularly deals.

stock option	Agreement granting a person the right to purchase stock in the future and at a fixed price.
stockholder	Shareholder in a corporation. (See "shareholder.")
stockholders' derivative action	See "shareholders' derivative action.
straw man	Person or entity having no actual interest in a property, business, or transaction, but appears as a party or principal in regard thereto (in name only), in place of a real-party who, for legitimate reasons or otherwise, does not wish his or her name to appear in that regard.
strict construction	Interpretation of the Constitution, or of a statute or rule, in the narrowest possible manner, inferring nothing which does not appear in the plain language thereof.
strict liability	Automatic responsibility, relieving plaintiff of burden of proof beyond defendant's manufacture or sale of a product and injury proximately resulting from that product. (See, "*res ipsa loquitur*," and "shift of burden.")
strike	(1) To delete from the court records, on spoken or written motion, all or a portion of a witness' testimony, or all or a portion of a filed pleading. (2) An organized protest by employees who refuse to work and who discourage others from patronizing their employer's business in an effort to obtain employment concessions from their employer in consideration for their returning to work.
structure	(1) Anything constructed on real property, from a birdbath to a skyscraper. (2) To formulate an agreement or transaction in a manner which permits it to go forward. *Viz.*, to structure a deal.

studio	Facility in which rehearsals or performances are conducted. Recording studios frequently have their own unique sound qualities, both as a function of their physical structure (ambience) and as a result of their electronic equipment and personnel. Selection of a particular recording studio may therefore be a creative factor in determining the ultimate sound of a finished recording.
sua sponte	Literally, "of its own will," *(Latin)* referring to actions taken by the court on its own initiative, without either party making a motion for such action.
sub rosa	Literally, "under the rose." *(Latin)* Confidential; secret; off the record; not to be repeated.
Subchapter S corporation	Option available to small, closely-held corporations, under a provision of the federal tax code (*i.e.,* 26 USC § 1366) which permits the shareholders to treat corporate profits as personal income, and to pay taxes accordingly. A corporation which does not qualify under Subchapter S is referred to as a "C corporation"
subcontractor	Person or business which contracts to provide goods or services in fulfillment of all or a portion of an obligation of another (the prime contractor) arising under a separate (prime) contract, to which the subcontractor is not a party.
sublease	Lease by a tenant to another (a subtenant) of all or a portion of property owned by (and leased from) another person or entity.
submitted	The turning over to the court, for its decision, a matter which has been fully briefed and argued. That which occurs when both sides have rested. At trial, questions of fact are then submitted to the jury for their deliberation.
subordinate	Causing a claim which has legal priority or over another claim to become junior to that other claim, either voluntarily or by court order.

subordination agreement	Written contract by which the holder of a claim entitled to priority over another claim agrees to subordinate that claim and become junior to the other claim.
suborning perjury	Crime of encouraging, inducing or assisting another in providing false testimony under oath or otherwise under penalty of perjury.
subpena	Alternative, modernized spelling of *subpoena*.
subpoena	Literally, "under [threat of] punishment." *(Latin)* Court order served upon a witness, commanding that witness to appear at a certain time and place to testify. Failure to obey is punishable as a contempt of court. Subpoenas are used to compel a person to appear in court or at a deposition.
subpoena duces tecum	Court order served upon a custodian of records, commanding that custodian to produce particular documents, or particular categories of documents, identified in the subpoena at a certain time and place, and may also command the custodian to testify as a witness in regard to those documents. Failure to obey is punishable as a contempt of court. *Subpoena duces tecum* is generally abbreviated by the acronym, "SAT."
subrogation	Substitution of one person or entity for another in regard to legal claims of the original claimant, the new party having advanced to the former party payment of all or a portion of the underlying claim. *E.g.,* when an insurance company pays its insured for a loss, the insurer obtains the insured's legal right to file suit against a person or entity liable for such loss.
subrogee	Person or entity that assumes another person's legal right to bring an action. (See "subrogation.")
subrogor	Person or entity that transfers his, her or its legal right to bring an action. (See "subrogation.")
subscribe (1)	Literally, to "write (sign) below." *(Latin)* To sign one's name to (*i.e.,* execute) a document.

subscribe (2)	To agree to purchase, as with an initial stock offering.
subscribe (3)	To accept as valid that which another has first advanced. (*E.g.*, to subscribe to another's beliefs.)
substantial performance	In contract law, fulfillment of the material and fundamental contract obligations, with any failure to perform consisting only of technical, minor or unimportant variances from a strict interpretation of the agreement. (See "partial performance.")
substantive evidence	Evidence offered to prove or disprove a material fact at issue, as distinct from evidence offered to discredit documentary evidence or witness' testimony (impeachment evidence), or to corroborate other evidence or testimony (corroborating evidence.)
substantive law	That portion of laws which creates, defines, and regulates rights, as distinct from "remedial law" which establishes enforcement methods to protect those rights and remedies for violation of those rights.
substitute	To change the legal representation of a party to a lawsuit. The new attorney is referred to as the "substitute attorney" or "substituting attorney," while former counsel is referred to as the "substituted attorney" Generally, the new attorney is said to "substitute in" (or "sub in") to the case, and the former attorney is said to have been "substituted out" ("subbed-out") of the case.
substituted service	Following diligent attempts at personal service of process (*e.g.*, 3 separate attempts), alternate service by delivery into the hands of a person of suitable age in apparent charge of premises which are the primary residence or place of business of the person or entity being served, followed by mailing a copy of the same documents to that same location, addressed to the person served. Proof of substituted service generally requires a declaration of diligence regarding the specific attempts at personal service made before substituted service.

substitution	Putting one person or thing in the in place of another, in particular replacement of litigation counsel.
substitution of attorney	Document by which party to a lawsuit changes counsel, generally requiring the signature of the party (expressing the desire to change counsel, as indicated), former counsel (acknowledging that he or she is being substituted out), and new counsel (agreeing to become new counsel of record.)
suffer	(1) To allow or permit. (2) To experience pain, anguish or distress, whether physical, mental or emotional.
suffering	The prolonged feeling or sensation which results from an experience which is painful, humiliating, or otherwise mentally, physically, or emotionally distressing.
suggested retail list price	An approximation of the price at which retailers will, on average, sell a product. Generally abbreviated by its acronym, "SRLP," it is used for a reference amount in negotiating artist's royalties. (See "royalty base" and "packaging charge.")
sui generis	Literally, "of its own kind." *(Latin)* One of a kind; unique; irreplaceable. Not fungible.
suit	Generic term for any complaint or petition.
sum certain	A precise amount, expressly stated in a contract or on the face of a negotiable instrument or other writing.
summary adjudication of issues	Also referred to (in some jurisdictions) as a "Partial Summary Judgment," a partial judgment with respect to only certain issues or cause(s) of action, based upon the court's finding that, based on matters of law and on facts which are not in dispute, the moving party is entitled to such judgment.

summary judgment	Judgment entered by the court, upon motion and the court's finding that, based on matters of law and on facts which are not in dispute, the moving party is entitled to judgment, without trial, as to the entire case.
summation	Counsel's final argument at the conclusion of trial, recapitulating what he or she believes the trial evidence and testimony has proven, prior to the matter being submitted for judgment.
summons	Official document issued by the court at the time a lawsuit is filed, commanding the defendant parties to respond within a specified number of days after being served. By virtue of the judicial power residing in it, the summons, upon being served, creates the legal foundation for the court's jurisdiction and authority over the person served.
sunset clause	Executory contract provision setting forth continuing rights and obligations of parties with respect to each other after termination of the contract.
supersedeas	Literally, "you shall desist." *(Latin)* A court order (writ)directed to a lower court, commanding that lower court to stop all further proceedings in a case, pending further order.
supplemental	Referring to something which is added. appended, attached, or annexed to something else for the purpose of completing, complementing, or facilitating it.
suppression of evidence	(1) Judicial determination to not allow certain evidence to be introduced or admitted. (See "preclusion.") (2) Act of extrinsic fraud when suppression or concealment of evidence is by party or counsel obligated to have produced such evidence. (See, "extrinsic fraud.")

supra	Literally, "above." *(Latin)* Used as an internal reference in pleadings, briefs, opinions and other writings, directing the reader's attention to something appearing earlier in the same document. *E.g.,* "The decision in <u>Jones v. Smith</u> (cited *supra*) states..."
supremacy clause	Provision of the U.S. Constitution (Article VI, clause 2) which states: *"This Constitution, and the Laws of the United States which shall be made in Pursuance thereof; and all Treaties made, or which shall be made, under the Authority of the United States, shall be the supreme Law of the Land; and the Judges in every State shall be bound thereby, any Thing in the Constitution or Laws of any state to the Contrary notwithstanding."* The supremacy clause requires that, in any conflict between federal law and state law, the state law must yield and that federal law governs. (See also, "preemption.")
Supreme Court	(1) The highest court of the United States, deriving its authority directly from the Constitution. Because of its unique power, the U.S. Supreme Court considers, but is not bound by, the doctrine of *stare decisis* and its own prior opinions. The ultimate court of last resort in the United States.
	(2) In most states (notably excluding New York), the name of the highest court of each state. The court of last resort, at the state level.
	(3) In New York, a trial court of original jurisdiction, equivalent to the Superior Court in most states. (In New York, the court of last resort is the state Court of Appeals.)
surcharge	(1) Additional (added) charge, tax, impost, fee, cost, or duty.
	(2) To impose such additional charge.
surety	Person or entity which guarantees performance or payment on behalf of another, in the event of failure of such performance or payment.
surplusage	In construing or analyzing legal documents, all language which is incidental or superfluous, rather than material or necessary.

surrebuttal	In legal argument and pleadings, a party's response to the other party's rebuttal. Generally only permitted if new matter is introduced in the course of the rebuttal. (See "order of argument" and "rebuttal.")
surrender	To turn over to another possession, custody or control of real or personal property.
surrogate	Person who acts in the place and stead of another person. A substitute.
surrogate's court	Court in some states (including New York) with limited jurisdiction over probate and adoption matters.
survivor	Person who outlives another.
survivorship	Right to receive full title or ownership upon the death of a joint tenant.
suspended sentence	Act of judicial clemency, in which penalty is announced, but its imposition is stayed, and the convicted defendant usually placed on probation with the further condition that, if the terms of probation are violated, the full sentence will then be imposed. (See, "probation.")
sustain	To support or affirm an evidentiary objection or certain types of motions. (*E.g.,* a demurrer is sustained or overruled, rather than granted or denied.) (See "overrule")
swear	To declare under oath that one's testimony will be true and complete. (See also, "oath" and "perjury")
sweetening	Process of modifying a completed recording by various means to enhance its sound qualities prior to its commercial release. This may include re-recording portions of the original, re-balancing tracks, addition of new elements, or the electronic removal or enhancement of existing elements.

swindle

(1) To defraud. Larceny by trick, misrepresentation, or other means of deception.

(2) A scheme which is intended to perpetrate a fraud.

sync license

Negotiated license to use a composition as part of an audiovisual presentation, such as a motion picture, music video, television program or commercial. Abbreviated form of "synchronization license." There is no standard or statutory fee.

synchronization rights

Right to synchronize music to visual images. Synchronization may require two separate licenses; a sync license from the copyright owner for the composition; and a master use license if a preexisting recording of that composition is to be used.

syndicate

(1) Association of persons and/or entities for the purpose of negotiating and concluding a particular business transaction. A joint venture.

(2) To form such an association.

T

T Bill   See "Treasury Bill."

tacit   Understood, implied or inferred, without having been specifically stated.

tacit admission   Failure to deny a statement or accusation which a reasonable person would deny. Conduct from which an admission or acquiescence regarding a particular statement may be reasonably inferred. Such failure or conduct may be legally interpreted as an admission that the subject statement or accusation is true274.

tainted evidence   Information which has been obtained through unlawful means, or derived from unlawfully obtained evidence. Unless it can be demonstrated that such information would have inevitably been discovered through other, lawful sources, it may be precluded from being introduced as evidence. (See "fruit of the poisonous tree")

take   (1) To obtain possession.

(2) In musical (audio) recording, any one of several sequentially-made live recordings of the same composition or portion of a composition, made by the same performer(s).

(3) In film or video recording, one of a several sequentially-made visual recordings of the same scene or portion of a scene.

(4) Colloquially, one's opinion on a particular event, occurrence or circumstance.

talent agent   Person or entity (talent agency) licensed to represent artists for the purpose of securing engagements for a fee based on a percentage of the sums received for such engagement. See "booking agent."

tangible property	Property which has actual, physical reality (*e.g.,* a chair, an astray, etc.) as distinguished from "intangible" property (*e.g.,* the goodwill of a business.) That which can be physically measured and located in place and time.
tax evasion	Crime of attempting to avoid, by fraud, payment of some of all taxes due.
tax	Levy (charge) of money imposed by government to finance itself and its expenditures. Almost anything can be the basis for taxation: income, sales, value, property, death, particular products, services, etc.
tax return	Form filed with taxing agency, reporting income, deductions, credits, and taxes owed (or refund due.)
tax sale	Forced public auction of taxpayer's property to satisfy unpaid tax obligations.
TD	Acronym for Trust Deed (or "deed of trust.")
technically satisfactory	Phrase used to establish delivery conditions for recordings, requiring merely that they be properly recorded and reproducible, without reference to their artistic merit.
temporary injunction	See "preliminary injunction" and "restraining order"
tenancy	Right of tenant to possession, use, and quiet enjoyment of real property, subject to performance of obligations of agreement by which tenant holds right. A possessory right.
tenancy at sufferance	Continuing tenancy after a lease or rental agreement has expired but before landlord has forced an eviction. A tenant at sufferance has no possessory right, but only bare possession.
tenancy at will	Permissive, continuing tenancy of property, without fixed term, as in a month-to-month tenancy.

tenancy in common	Form of ownership of property by two or more persons, each ow whom owns a discrete but undivided interest in the property which interest is independently conveyable and inheritable. Principally distinguished from "joint tenancy," in which a co-owner's interest cannot be separately alienated, but passes to surviving co-owner(s) at death. Unless an agreement between them provides to the contrary, any tenant-in-common may sell his or her interest to a third party. (See "buy-sell agreement.")
tenant	Person who occupies real property owned by another, pursuant to a lease or rental agreement, or subsequent to expiration of such lease or agreement.
tender	An offer of value, without further condition. The actual proffer of value, rather than the promise to do so. Tender immediately precedes delivery, which occurs the instant recipient accepts possession of the tender. Note that U.S. currency declares on its face that it is "legal tender" which can pe proffered to another as payment.
tenement	In its broadest legal sense, now archaic, anything which can be freely owned. Commonly, tenement now refers to houses and other buildings used primarily for residential purposes.
tenure	A right, term, and/or method of holding. In real property, the right to hold title, and the period of time during which it has been held. A tenant's tenure is the term of the lease. An elected official's tenure is the period of time during which he or she holds office. A "tenured" professor is one who has obtained a contract of effectively-permanent employment. *Etc.*
term	(1) Period of time during which a contract is to remain in effect. A fixed period.
	(2) The period of time during which something continues. (*E.g.*, term of office; a jail term; term of pregnancy.)
	(3) A word or phrase.

terminate	To end. Put a stop to. Conclude a term. To fire or discharge an employee.
termination	The act of terminating something.
term of art	Phrase or word which has a specialized or precise meaning within the usage and custom of a particular field or profession, generally different from a common meaning which those same words may have in general usage.
territory	An assigned geographical or geopolitical location. In licencing, the licence may be "worldwide" or limited to a particular territory (*e.g.,* the U.S., Europe, Sweden, *etc.*)
testamentary	Referring to a will.
testify	To give oral evidence (testimony) under oath or upon affirmation.
testimony	Oral evidence given by a witness under oath or upon affirmation.
theft	General term for any crime in which a person takes or retains possession of the property of another without right or permission.
thence	(1) From that place; from there. (*E.g.,* I'll be going from here to the clerk's office, and thence to court.) (2) From that circumstance or source; therefrom. (*E.g.,* Thence came a number of complications.) (*Cf.,* "hence" and "whence.")
thenceforth	From that moment forward in time. From then on. (*Cf.,* "henceforth")
therefor	For that; for it. *E.g.,* "The court issued the order because good cause appeared therefor."

therefore	For that reason; for that cause. Consequently. Used to introduce a logical conclusion. *E.g.*, "I am busy, and therefore cannot attend."
thereon	Upon this, that, or it. *E.g.*, "It is important to get a signed release. Your success may depend thereon."
theretofore	Prior to a certain date, time or occurrence. *E.g.*, "The company was incorporated in June 2003. Theretofore, it had operated as a partnership."
thereupon	(1) Concerning some particular matter. *E.g.,* "They spoke thereupon for several hours." (2) Immediately following or concurrently with some occurrence. *E.g.*, "When payment has been received, you shall thereupon deliver title to the new owner."
third party	Any person who is not party to a contract or a transaction. One not directly in privity.
third-party beneficiary	Person not party to a contract but who has a beneficial interest in that contract and therefore a lawful right to bring suit in respect to that contract.
tie-in	Form of merchandising or promotion in which an artist's or project's name and likeness are used in connection with a commercial product which is otherwise unrelated to that artist or project. Tie-ins are distinct from endorsements (where an artist's name is used to advertise a product ostensibly used professionally by the artist) and from merchandising (where the product is actually centered around the artist or project.)
time is of the essence	Phrase used in contracts to indicate that the timeliness of performance is itself a material, bargained for consideration of the agreement, and lateness may be considered a material breach.
time served	Period of time during which a criminal defendant has been in jail, usually while awaiting trial.

timely	On time. Within the period of time allowed.
title insurance	Insurance policy which guarantees to the real property purchaser that title to that property is being conveyed without any undisclosed encumbrances or claims clouding its title.
title	Ownership of real or personal property.
title report	Written history of the title record of property, showing all encumbrances and the chain of title.
to wit	"That is." Used to preface an example or definition which illustrates or elaborates upon the preceding statement. *Example:* "An officer of the company, to wit; its president."
toll	(1) to delay, suspend or stay the effect of a statute, particularly a statute of limitations. (2) A fee charged for use of something, usually a road, highway, bridge, or similar work of construction.
tools of trade	Such equipment as is necessary to performance of a person's occupation.
tort	A civil wrong. *E.g.,* the crime of theft is also the tort of conversion, for which a civil remedy exists.
tort claims act	Laws which establish particular required procedures as a prerequisite to filing suit against a government entity, usually involving a very limited period of time in which one must act.
tortfeasor	Person who commits a tort.
tortious	Having the elements or quality of a tort.
tour	Live performances by an artist or group, or by several artist or groups, appearing in several different cities over an extended period of time.

tour support	Financial and logistical commitment by record company or other interested party to assist in presentation of a series of live performances by an artist or group. A guarantee of tour support may appear as a negotiated provision within a recording contract.
trade	(1) Any business or occupation for profit. (2) To exchange one property for another. To barter. (3) To buy and sell securities.
trade name	Name of a business or of its product(s), which by its continued use has acquired general recognition and hence become a valuable property of that business.
trade secret	Process, method, plan, formula or other information unique to a particular business and the value of which is dependent, in whole or in part, upon its remaining secret.
trademark	Distinctive emblem, design, logo, typestyle, or visual representation used by a business. Trademarks may be registered, and thereafter utilize the circle-R ("®") emblem. Unregistered trademarks may use the "TM" symbol.
transaction	Any activity involving two or more parties or things in which both or all parties are affected or influenced in some way by that activity. (Note: In Louisiana, "transaction" has a special, defined legal meaning, generally equivalent to "accord and satisfaction." See "Napoleonic Code.")
transcript	Written record of all proceedings in court, deposition, or other proceeding which is reported stenographically.
transcription license	Agreement granting permission to use composition for public audio (radio) broadcast. (*Cf.,* "Synchronization License.")
transfer	Change of possession or ownership of property from one person or entity to another.

treasurer	Chief financial officer (CFO) of a corporation or other organization.
treasury bond	Long-term, interest bearing bond issued by the U.S. Treasury.
treasury bill	Short term promissory note issued by the U.S. Treasury for terms of 3, 6 or 12 months, in multiples of $10,000. Treasury bills (or T-Bills) do not bear interest, but are sold at a discount.
treasury note	Medium term (1-5 year) promissory note issued by the U.S. Treasury, bearing interest payable by coupon.
treasury stock	Shares of corporate stock which are owned by the corporation itself.
treaty	An agreement between sovereign nations. Treaties to which the United States is signatory, and which have been ratified by Congress, have the force of law. (See, "supremacy clause.")
treble damages	Three times the amount of actual damages, which may be awarded as punitive or exemplary damages when authorized by statute.
trespass	The act of entering onto another's property without permission.
trial	Adversarial proceeding presided over by a judge, with or without a jury, in which disputes of fact and law are presented, argued, and generally resolved in favor of one party or the other.
trial court	A court which conducts trials, as opposed to a court of appeal which reviews the actions of trial courts.

trial _de novo_	(1) Literally, a new trial.
	(2) Examination by an appellate court of the facts and evidence of a case, on the merits, for the purpose of determining the correctness of the trial court's judgment.
	(3) After non-binding arbitration, a subsequent judicial re-trial of the same issues, initiated by the party dissatisfied with the result of arbitration. .
tribunal	Any court, judicial body, or board which has judicial or quasi-judicial powers.
trier of fact	The judge or, in matters tried by jury, the jury, responsible for weighing the evidence presented and coming to a conclusion as to the facts of the case.
TRO	Acronym for Temporary Restraining Order.
true bill	Written decision of a Grand Jury, attesting to its having found that there is sufficient evidence to issue a criminal indictment in a particular case.
trust	Entity created to hold, receive, invest, distribute and otherwise use assets for specific, stated purposes and for the benefit of persons named as beneficiaries. A trust may be either revocable or irrevocable.
trust deed	See "deed of trust."
trust fund	The principal (_corpus_) of a trust, consisting of its initial capital, plus its subsequent interest and investment income and holdings. Depending upon the terms of the trust, beneficiaries may be entitled to receive regular income, or other disbursements, from the trust fund.
trustee	Person or entity who controls the assets (_corpus_) of a trust, in a fiduciary capacity, for the benefit of the beneficiaries and under guidelines established by the settlor in creating the trust.
trustor	Settlor. The creator of a trust.

tune	The musical portion of a song, as distinct from its lyrics.
turnaround	Return of masters or compositions to the original owner or artist, generally at a point in time fixed by contract, or based upon non-use by the possessor. See "reversion."
typo	A typographical error.

U

ubiquitous   Pervasive. Always present.

UCC   Acronym for Uniform Commercial Code.

UCC-1   A recordable financing agreement by which a lien is voluntarily created against personal property (chattels), to secure an obligation.

UCMJ   Acronym for the Uniform Code of Military Justice, a federal code which governs the conduct of U.S. military personnel in all branches of service.

ultimate fact   Fact essential to adjudication of an issue. Fact which it is expected that evidence will support. Conclusive fact.

ultra   Beyond. Outside of. In excess of. *(Latin)*

ultra vires   Literally, "beyond powers," refers to any action which is beyond the lawful authority of the person taking such action.

ulterior motive   Having a purpose other than or beyond the stated or obvious purpose. A hidden intention or agenda.

umbrella   Something which covers numerous other things. A contract, policy, or provision which supplements other such writings by addressing circumstances which exhaust the remedies provided by those others. *E.g.* an "umbrella" insurance policy provides separate coverage for unspecified losses which are in excess of coverage limits of other, existing policies.

unclean hands   An affirmative defense based on legal doctrine which states that the court will not grant equitable relief to a plaintiff or petitioner who has committed wrongful acts in the course of the occurrence or transaction underlying the complaint or petition. The doctrine applies only when the wrongdoing has a proximate relationship to the subject matter in dispute.

unconscionable   (1) Any intentional act or conduct which is grossly unfair to another person, and shocking to the conscience of an average person.

(2) In a contract, that which is manifestly unfair to one party, and unreasonably beneficial to another, under circumstances where the lesser party was afforded no meaningful or informed choice in accepting such conditions. Unconscionable provisions include, but are not necessarily limited to, gross overall one-sidedness in disclaiming warranty, limiting damages, or obtaining procedural advantages. An unconscionable contract may also be inferred from fact that one-sided provisions are obscured through use of small print or effectively-unintelligible language, or where the lesser party is particularly susceptible.

unconstitutional   Anything which violates the provisions, protections or guarantees embodied in the United States Constitution or its amendments, or the Constitutions of any of the several states, or their amendments. In particular, referring to any action of the state or federal governments, or of governmental representatives, or a statute, regulation, rule, judgment, court order or opinion, which violates a Constitutional provision, protection, or guaranty.

underwriter   Person or entity which agrees, for consideration, to become financially liable up to a maximum amount and up until a certain date, should certain occurrences, in fact, occur in the course of some particular undertaking. Underwriters are the persons responsible for payment in the event of an insurance claim. Underwriters are also involved in the issuance of securities. (See, "IPO.")

undisclosed principal	Person who is a real party but who acts through an agent and whose identity is not revealed by that agent to other interested partes.
undivided interest	The interest of a co-owner of property, wherein the nature of the property renders it indivisible. *I.e.,* a proportional interest in the whole of something, rather than complete ownership of a particular portion of that thing. *E.g.,* a 50% ownership of a racehorse, rather than complete ownership of half of a (dead) horse. Particularly applied in real property owned in common with others.
undue influence	Any wrongful or improper persuasion of another to induce him or her to act in a manner other than he or she would have acted without such persuasion. Exercise of influence which deprives another of free choice. Most frequently found in cases where the person exercising such persuasion is in a special position of trust or influence over another who is infirm, moribund, in distress, weakened, overwrought, or otherwise in a state of mind which is particularly suggestible or subject to being directed by the will of another.
unfair competition	Generally, any act of dishonest, misleading or fraudulent nature which adversely affects the business of a rival. Particularly, efforts to substitute one's own products or services for those of a competitor in a market where that competitor has established a good reputation, by use of confusingly similar names, packaging, advertising, or other means which have a deceptive effect on consumers.
unfair trade practices	Prohibited business conduct which improperly interferes with a competing product or service, or which has the effect of confusing or misleading the public in respect to such competing product or service. (See "Lanham Act")

Uniform Codes	Proposed codes (laws) written by the National Conference of Commissioners on Uniform State Laws. The Uniform Codes are divided into those areas of law which each addresses (*e.g.*, the "Uniform Consumer Credit Code.") None of the Uniform Codes have been fully adopted by <u>all</u> states, but they nonetheless provide useful guidelines for consideration by state legislators in crafting their own state laws.
Uniform Commercial Code	Statutes governing the conduct of business transactions. The Uniform Commercial Code (commonly referred to by the acronym "UCC") has been substantially adopted by 49 states, Louisiana being the exception.
unilateral	By one person or entity, acting alone.
unissued stock	Shares of corporate stock which have authorized by its charter and/or articles of incorporation, but have never been issued. Although generally held in the form of blank stock certificates by the corporation's Treasurer or Secretary, they are distinct from "treasury shares" which have been previously issued and then repurchased by the corporation.
unjust enrichment	Benefit obtained by one party, at the expense of another, through chance, mistake or that other's misfortune. Equitable doctrine which demands that the party receiving such benefits make restitution to the party suffering thereby.
unlawful	That which is in violation of a statute.
unlawful detainer	(1) Possession of real property without right. (2) A cause of action to secure lawful possession of property from a person holding possession without right, and for damages, through an expedited legal process.
unliquidated	Something of value which has not been converted into money, or as to which the monetary value has not been calculated or agreed.

unrecouped	Album or project which has not earned sufficient revenue to offset advances and other accrued expenses.
uplift	British synonym for "markup." Uplift is frequently applied as a factor to adjust wholesale (PPD, BPD) prices and royalties based on that price.
URAA	Acronym for the "Uruguay Round Agreements Act" which was enacted by Congress to implement the General Agreement on Tariffs and Trade (GATT). The URAA amended U.S. copyright law to bring it into closer conformity with copyright protections afforded in other countries.
USD	Acronym for "United States Dollars" used to clarify the currency intended in contracts or negotiable instruments. The familiar "$" (dollar) symbol is now used to denote the currency of several countries (*e.g.*, Australia, Canada), although that symbol was originally derived by superimposing a narrow "U" over the letter "S."
use	(1) Right to enjoy the benefits of property. (2) Possession of such property and concurrent enjoyment of such right.
usurious	Referring to any transactions which includes an interest rate exceeding the legal maximum interest rate, unless the transaction, or the party charging such interest, is legally exempt from such maximum rate.
usurp	To take over the authority, rights, office, privileges, or property of another, without right, through guile or by force.
usury	The charging of an interest rate in excess of the legal interest rate, without lawful exemption to such restriction.

V

vacate

(1) To set aside or annul a court order or judgment.

(2) To remove oneself from tenancy, occupancy, or possession.

valuable consideration

A necessary element of any valid contract, which confers a benefit from one party to the other, in exchange for value (consideration) received in return.

variance

(1) The fact or quality of being different or inconsistent.

(2) The state of disagreeing or quarreling.

(3) A discrepancy between two statements or documents. That which diverges from what was originally intended, promised, agreed or understood.

(4) An exemption granted in regard to a regulation or ordinance, particularly in regard to zoning laws.

vend

To sell.

vendee

A buyer.

vendor

A seller.

venire

List of names of person summoned for jury duty, from which jurors may be selected.

venireman (venireperson)

A member of the panel of potential jurors interviewed by the court during the *voire dire* process.

venture capital

Capital invested in a project in which there is a substantial element of risk. In consequence of that risk, venture capital arrangements often require that the investor receive a substantial ownership interest in the project (equity financing) as well as preferential recoupment of the investment.

venue	(1) The location in which a legal proceeding is conducted. (2) Colloquially, the location in which any event takes place. (3) The club, theater or auditorium in which a concert or other entertainment is presented.
verb. sap.	Abbreviation of the Latin phrase, "*verbum sapienti*" ("A word to the wise [is enough.]") Used in reference to a "friendly" warning or caveat.
verbal	In words.
verbal contract	Often used erroneously as a synonym for "oral contract," a verbal contract is one which has been expressed in words, whether oral or written, as distinguished from an "implied contract."
verdict	The decision of a jury (or of a judge, sitting without a jury) upon the facts, after a trial. To become final, a jury's verdict must be accepted by the court, which has the power to set the jury's verdict aside under certain circumstances. (See "NOV.")
verification	Declaration under oath or penalty of perjury that a preceding writing is true, correct and accurate, based upon the attesting person's personal knowledge or (if so stated) upon information received and his or her belief in the truth thereof.
versus	Literally, "against." *(Latin)* Abbreviated as "vs." or "v." or "-v-" in legal pleadings and case citations.
vest	To have absolute right to title, ownership or interest in a property, right or benefit.
vested	Referring to one's right, title, ownership or interest having been duly established as being absolute.
vexatious litigant	A person who files a lawsuit with knowledge that there is no legal basis for such suit.

vicarious liability	Indirect legal responsibility for the acts of another. Liability which is imputed from circumstances or situation, rather than from the actions or negligence of the person held liable. (See *"respondent superior."*)
vice versa	Literally, "in turned position." The other way around. Used to indicate positional reverse of the main items in a preceding list or statement.
vinyl	Referring to analogue phonograph records (*i.e.,* 45-rpm, 78-rpm, and 33⅓-rpm LPs) which were formerly the primary media for commercial music releases.
viz.	Contraction of *"videlicet." (Latin)* Namely; that is; to wit. Used similarly to *"i.e."*
vocalist	A singer.
vocals	That portion of a musical performance or recording which consists of human voices.
void	(1) Generally, without form or substance. Empty.
	(2) That which is wholly without legal force or effect. A void agreement is to be distinguished from a "voidable" agreement. (see "voidable.")
	(3) To cancel or annul. To make something to be without legal force or effect, either voluntarily, or by court order, or by legislative or executive action.
void *ab initio*	That which is void, or is made void, from its very beginning, as though it had never happened.
voidable	That which can be declared void by reason of legal defects.

voir dire	To speak truly. (French) *Voire dire* is a process of examination by which jurors and witnesses may be examined by the court and the attorneys to ascertain their qualifications to serve or testify. Generally, *voire dire* is used as a synonym for "jury selection," although the process has other applications, particularly with respect to ascertaining the qualifications of proposed expert witnesses.
voluntary settlement conference	In litigation, a court proceeding requested by one or more of the parties, in which the parties attempt to resolve disputes prior to trial. Generally such conferences are presided over by a judge other than the judge who will try the case. Often referred to by the acronym "VSC."
vs.	Standard abbreviation of "versus."

W

w/	Standard abbreviation for "with."
w/o	Standard abbreviation for "without."
waive	To voluntarily give up a right, privilege or benefit to which one is or may be entitled. This may be done expressly, or may be implied by actions, or inferred from inaction.
waiver	The voluntary giving up of a right, privilege or benefit, either knowingly and informedly, or through an inference which may be drawn from one's conduct.
wanton	Malicious. Reckless. Done without thought, conscience, or consideration of consequences.
ward	(1) To guard, protect, or fend off. (2) A minor or incompetent person who has been placed in the care of a guardian by the court. (3) A political subdivision of some cities and towns. A precinct. A constituency.
warrant	(1) To justify or provide good cause or reason. To merit. (2) In contract, to promise that a certain material statement or representation of facts is true. (3) A written order, signed by a judge, granting authority to a governmental agency (*e.g.,* the police) to undertake a specified task (*e.g.,* conduct a search of a particular location, or arrest a particular person.) (4) A written order by any government authority which delegates specified and limited authority to another, by virtue of which that other may then act.

warranties and representations	That portion of a contract in which a party recites certain facts, represents that such facts are true, and assures the other party that those facts may be relied upon. In recording contracts, these generally relate to ownership of a group name, copyright ownership, and full disclosure of any prior, competing obligations.
warranty	(1) A promise that some particular statement of material fact is true.
	(2) A written statement by a manufacturer or seller of goods or services, at the time of sale, assuring the buyer that those goods or services have particular qualities upon which the buyer may rely.
	(3) In certain circumstances, a promise of suitability and/or quality of goods or services which will be legally presumed, even in the absence of a written or spoken promise to that effect. (*I.e.*, an "implied warranty.")
waste	Abuse or destructive use of property by one who is in lawful possession of that property. Neglect or misuse of one's own property.
watered stock	Corporate stock which is issued without the corporation receiving its full value in payment. Usually issued as a bonus or in payment for services, the issuance of such stock dilutes (waters down) the value of all previously issued shares.
webcasting	Public distribution of audio and/or video works over the internet. Contraction of [World Wide] Web + [broad]casting. (See "Digital Millennium Copyright Act.")
weight of evidence	The credibility and relevant value of evidence presented to support a proposition of fact in a matter at issue.
well	Portion of courtroom between the judge's bench and counsels' table. The well is not to be entered or crossed by anyone without express permission of the court.

well settled	A legal premise or rule which is so well established and understood within the legal community as to require no further authority.
whence	From where or from which. From what place. From what origin or source. (*Cf.,* "hence" and "thence.")
whereas	Because. Used to introduce a statement of fact, as in the recitals of a contract. *E.g.,* "Whereas, John Doe is the owner of certain property; and Whereas, Richard Roe is desirous of acquiring that property..."
wherefor	For that purpose. The cause or intention underlying an action or situation. *E.g.,* "The Court found that good cause existed to enjoin defendant from continuing operations, wherefor a restraining order was issued." (*Cf.,* "wherefore.")
wherefore	(1) For which reason. Used to introduce a conclusion which logically follows from prior statements. *E.g.,* following the recitals of a contract, "Wherefore the parties do hereby agree as follows:..." (*Cf.,* "wherefor.") (2) Why? (*Archaic.*)
whereupon	At which time, or at the time of such occurrence. *E.g.,* "The purchaser shall deliver payment to escrow, whereupon the escrow officer shall deliver title to the purchaser."
wherewithal	Capability. Particularly financial ability to perform.
white collar crime	Colloquial term for financial crimes which involve no violence, but which are committed through commercial fraud, embezzlement, or other means of diverting funds, often through abuse of some position of trust. (See "fiduciary duty.")
will contest	Lawsuit which challenges the terms of a will, or which questions the validity of the entire will.
will	Written document which states how a person wishes to have his or her assets distributed after death.

willful	Conscious; intentional; by design.
wind down	The process of bringing business operations to a final conclusion, over a period of time. (See "wind up" and "sunset clause.")
wind up	To conclude the operations of a business, liquidating its assets and settling its obligations. (See "wind down" and "sunset clause.")
WIPO	World Intellectual Property Organization. A specialized agency of the United Nations which promotes international use and protection of intellectual property. With its headquarters in Geneva, Switzerland, WIPO administers twenty-three international treaties dealing with different aspects of intellectual property protection. (See also, "DMCA.")
withdrawal	The voluntary removal of one's self (or of some thing) from a circumstance, position, transaction, agreement, proceedings, or other matter of which previously a part.
without limitation	Phrase used to expand stated provisions beyond what is expressly listed, and to thereby potentially include matter which is not included, *per se*.
witness	(1) One who has personal knowledge of facts relevant to a matter under consideration or at-issue. (2) One who has personally observed some incident or occurrence. (3) One who gives testimony under oath at a proceeding. (*Cf.,* "expert witness.")
words of art	Phrases or words which have a specialized meaning within a particular field or profession, generally different from a common meaning which those same words may have in general usage. Terms of art.

work for hire	A work which has been created by a person employed for that purpose, and the registered owner of which is that person's employer. Under copyright law, a work for hire occurs only when creation of the work falls within the normal course and scope of a regular employee's duties, or when there is a specific "work for hire" agreement for that particular work.
work for hire provision	Specific contract language stating that work created pursuant to the contract is "work for hire," and that copyright consequently vests in the hiring party, rather than the actual creator.
work product	All writings, notes, memoranda, drafts, reports, calendar notations, tape recordings, research, and other writings of every and any kind created or used in developing a final, published product. In law, every writing leading up to, but not including, any published pleading. Attorney's work product enjoys a special privilege of protection from disclosure similar to the attorney-client privilege regarding communications. Although an attorney may not suppress evidence, he or she cannot disclose materials which reflect his or her investigations, research, theories, impressions, considerations and thought processes which have led to whatever position is ultimately adopted.
Workers' Compensation	A state-mandated form of insurance covering workers injured in job-related accidents. In some states the state itself is the insurer; in other states such insurance must be acquired from commercial insurance firms. Insurance rates are based on a number of factors including salaries, firm history and risk of occupation. In many jurisdictions, a worker's compensation claim is the only remedy allowed to an employee for work-related injury claims against an employer.
writ of mandate	Also known as a writ of mandamus. A court order to a government agency, including a lower court, requiring or prohibiting some specific action.
writ	A written court order requiring specific action by the person or persons to whom it is directed.

wrongful termination

Cause of action brought by a former employee against a former employer for damages, based on allegation that employment was terminated for an unlawful purpose or by unlawful means, or pursuant to discriminatory policies or practices. (See "employee at will.")

X

x

(1) Shorthand abbreviation for "by," used when stating dimensions. or quantities. *E.g.,* "4 feet x 12 feet."

(2) Shorthand abbreviation for "times," used when stating quantities or in a mathematical equation.

(3) Lawyers' shorthand for "cross-" as in cross-examination or cross-defendant (*e.g.,* "x-Δ")

X

(1) Used on documents to indicate the place at which a signature is to be subscribed.

(2) Common mark used in lieu of a signature by those unable to sign their own names. Such subscription is generally valid if duly witnessed.

xerography

Photocopying process in which a negative image formed by a dry, powdered toner on an electrically charged surface is transferred onto paper or other material and then thermally fused onto it as a permanent, positive image.

Y

¥

Currency symbol denoting Japanese yen.

yellow dog clause

Illegal contract provision by which an employee agrees that he or she will not join a union.

yeas and nays

Tally of votes by a legislative or other democratic body, with the "yeas" being votes in the affirmative and the "nays" being votes in the negative with respect to the matter voted upon.

yield

(1) To surrender, relinquish, or withdraw. To give up.

(2) The rate at which an investment produces income.

Z

zero tolerance

Policy provision which states that no violation of an underlying policy or regulation will go unpunished. Theoretically, a person violating a policy which has a "zero tolerance" provision is immediately suspended or terminated from his or her employment, prosecuted, or subjected to such other penalty as the policy dictates, without being afforded a "second chance." The adoption and strict adherence to such a policy may help shield an employer from liability with respect to third-party claims. (See *"respondent superior."*)

zone

A defined area, generally distinguished by certain common traits or characteristics.

zone of privacy

Those areas of each person's life in which there is a reasonable expectation of privacy which may not be invaded by the public, the press, or by governmental agencies without due process. The extent of this zone of privacy varies based on the character of the person asserting it. *E.g.,* a "public figure" has a smaller zone of privacy than does an "ordinary" person. See "public figure."

AFTERWORD

Jackson Pollock is reported to have said, "True art lies in knowing when to stop." I hope I haven't gone beyond that point. I keep thinking, "What have I left out?," and I'm certain that several dozen words and phrases will occur to me within minutes after delivering this manuscript to the publisher.

I wrote the foreword to this book nearly a year ago, when I thought it was virtually complete and would only need a little tweaking. A day or two at most I was certain. Well, now it finally *is* finished, for better or worse, and I sincerely hope that it proves useful to readers throughout the music industry, both inside and outside of Business Affairs.

Any suggestions about words, phrases or definitions that might be added or changed in future editions will receive my grateful attention. Correspondence should be addressed to:

> Robert J. Nathan
> c/o Music Business Program
> Musicians' Institute
> 1621 N. McCadden Place
> Hollywood, California 90028

Since I began this Afterword with a quote on the nature of art, let me close with a tongue-in-cheek insight into artists' motivation from British actor, comedian, author (and lawyer), John Cleese:

> "Even if these ideas are only one-hundredth as
> intriguing to you as they were to me, I shall still
> get the royalties."

Thanks.

> — Robert J. Nathan
> Beverly Hills, California
> August 6, 2005

* * * * *

P.S.   I just went back and added another twenty-seven definitions. Mr. Pollock would *not* be pleased. (8-12-2005)

* * * * *

P.P.S.   My thanks to everyone who responded to the foregoing invitation. I've now added another nine pages. Sisyphus, move over! (8-25-2006)

NOTES

NOTES

NOTES